DEAD MATTER

DEAD MATTER

The Meaning of Iconic Corpses

Margaret Schwartz

UNIVERSITY OF MINNESOTA PRESS

Minneapolis · London

Published by the University of Minnesota Press
111 Third Avenue South, Suite 290
Minneapolis, MN 55401-2520
http://www.upress.umn.edu

Library of Congress Cataloging-in-Publication Data

Schwartz, Margaret.
    Dead matter : the meaning of iconic corpses / Margaret Schwartz.
    Includes bibliographical references and index.
    ISBN 978-0-8166-9433-4 (hc)
    ISBN 978-0-8166-9434-1 (pb)
    1. Dead—Social aspects. 2. Dead—History. 3. Aesthetic distance.
I. Title.
GT3150.S39   2015
306.9—dc23   2014046944

Printed in the United States of America on acid-free paper

The University of Minnesota is an equal-opportunity educator and employer.

21 20 19 18 17 16 15   10 9 8 7 6 5 4 3 2 1

For Harold Schwartz, who will never read this book,
and for Tillie, who someday might

CONTENTS

Preface   ix

Introduction: An Iconography of the Flesh   1

1. The Body of the Nation: Abraham Lincoln,
   Vladimir Lenin, and Eva Perón   27

2. Martyred Bodies: Emmett Till and Hamza al-Khateeb   53

3. Tabloid Bodies: Princess Diana and Michael Jackson   83

Conclusion: Communicating with the Corpse   103

Acknowledgments   113

Notes   117

Index   135

PREFACE

When I was fifteen, my father suffered a cardiac arrest and died at home, on the sofa bed in his office. This, my first and only experience with a corpse, sits at the heart of this book.

The corpse was recognizably my father, his face somewhat contorted in an expression anywhere between irritation and pain. His mouth and eyes were open. I remember grasping instantly that this body both was and was not my father. In retrospect, it surprises me that this should have been so, but to see him was to know instantly that it was he, and that he was dead. I remember feeling that there must be something one does when faced with a moment of such dramatic import. Something had happened to me, something that couldn't be undone. And so, like the moody, dramatic teenager I was, I reached not into my backlog of experience, which was negligible, but into my experience of pop culture. What do young girls in the movies do when their fathers unexpectedly die? I leaned over and kissed his forehead. For the first millisecond of contact, it felt normal. His skin had not changed in texture, and it was not yet cold. But something felt appallingly different as my lips touched his forehead. There was no response, nothing there. And then, as I remember it, something rose up from below, something utterly foreign and strange that made me withdraw. I didn't touch the corpse again, and soon the paramedics would come, and I wouldn't see him again until the viewing at the funeral home.

My father was a secular Jew who had left no instructions in the event of his death. Our family, shocked and grieving, simply followed the only script available in small-town Maine, where we lived far from extended family and outside the confines of any particular religious tradition: a funeral home, a gravestone, a public viewing. Later there would be a memorial, but not until scattered family members could assemble. The funeral home viewing was not a family or a religious experience but a public one, in every sense. I dressed up and encountered schoolmates and their parents. Yet again, I had no idea what this role was about.

The corpse as I first found it was awesome, sublime: it was to witness the imprint of an encounter with another world. It was the face of someone who has departed. This was nothing compared with the violation I felt looking at his embalmed and prepared corpse. Whatever they had done to my father had made him grotesque and horrible and wrong. It simply was not him. It was not even him dead. It was something else. The trauma of the corpse was the coincidence of familiarity and otherness—the undeniable sense that this loved someone is irrevocably elsewhere and otherwise. The embalmed corpse was an abomination. I couldn't stand to look at it; I felt ashamed that it should be displayed because I didn't want anyone to see him that way—with rouge on his cheeks and his lips and hands not-quite-discreetly stitched in place.

This was my emotional response in the moment. I don't mean to suggest that the unprepared corpse was "natural" or pure in some absolute way as compared to the artifice of the embalmed and prepared corpse. Those are academic distinctions, and this book was written to explore and justify the ideological investments in those kinds of claims. What I mean to highlight was the shocking difference between what I had assumed would be essentially the same body. In other words, it wasn't the fact of death alone that made the embalmed body upsetting to me. Something enormous had intervened between the moment of death and the moment of what I would now call the representation of death. At the time it felt like a denial of death, to paint him and arrange his limbs, his face and hands fixed in gestures he would never have used in life.

This book is part of years of struggle to understand that reaction. I have sought to make sense of what I saw and felt in the context of the only cosmology I know: of books, social theory, the Marxist traditions my relatives adopted when they arrived in this country from Eastern Europe and bequeathed to me in the form of an immigrant's dream of a liberal arts education.

In the nearly twenty-five years since I lost my father, I have struggled daily with how to grieve in a world where grieving is a lost art. It strikes me that I am not alone in this.

In such a world, we turn to what Kittler called the "realm of the dead" and Bazin called "embalmed time" and Sontag knew were memento mori: photographs. It wasn't only his body that changed when he died. His image changed too; every photograph of him in life seemed to carry within it the seeds of his early death. Trying to express this, I once digitized some home movies with the thought of making a (very awkward) short film. I am fifteen, and it's my first day of school, the September before he died. I pass across the camera's frame with the studied insouciance of adolescence, head down, laden with book and gym bags. With indescribable grace, my father pivots along the angle of my passage. "So long," he says.

AN ICONOGRAPHY OF THE FLESH

The realm of the dead is as extensive as the storage and transmission capabilities of a given culture.
FRIEDRICH KITTLER, *Gramophone, Film, Typewriter*

Dead bodies are material things that bear a referential relationship to an absent subject. They are a kind of medium that connects the living to the memory of a deceased. As such, they are the perfect starting point to what Bill Brown has termed a "materialist analysis of media."[1] The corpse is a material thing freighted with immensely powerful cultural meaning. To look at death practices from the starting point of the corpse is thus to inquire precisely into the relationship between the material and the textual, between the thing itself and the rich variety of representational texts required to make sense of it; it is to venture between the world of specific cultural and historical practice and the universality of death. A materialist analysis of media begins with the corpse because the corpse is itself a complex figure of mediation.

This book outlines a theory of the corpse as a communicative object. I am particularly interested in how the corpse's physical materiality—the existential and biological fact of death, which is linked to the corpse's status as thing—interacts with the image. Analyzing this interaction allows a third way to parse the difference between the body as something performed and textual and the body as a mute, ineffable, veiled "thing in itself." To theorize the body not as experience or agency but as flesh, as material thing, requires a different kind of vocabulary, one not dependent on subjectivity or intention nor reducible to signification or language. This book is an attempt to sketch such a vocabulary.

Ritual practices surrounding the corpse constitute this figuring of a relationship between the material world and signification. They forge a kind of mediation or tell a kind of story about what is being remembered here, in this way, through this flesh, this monument, this absence. How we prepare the corpse, how we lay it to rest, and how we mark the space of its passing are all highly symbolic practices that construct a contingent understanding of death, memory, and the meaning of life. These practices articulate cultural values: they narrate legacy, they affirm identity and continuity, and they provide a space for the memory of the deceased. They do so, however, with a material object as the centerpiece: the practices themselves account for and contextualize the movement of this thing from *here,* from the present, to the *there* of memory, afterlife, legacy.

Furthermore, images of the corpse have been used in popular and devotional art for centuries to invoke the fleeting vanity of the living body.[2] Corpses may symbolize the power of the state, as in public executions, or the wrongful and horrible abuse of that power, as with photographs of atrocity. The corpse functions as an archetypical symbol of human finality, of the power of death as something that always threatens subjectivity from elsewhere, always destabilizes the present with the threat of flux, decay, disappearance, and oblivion.

Wherever the corpse appears, then, it both figures and is a literal figure of a relation: between life and death, this life and the next, the present and the future perfect of memory. The corpse is a literal figure for mediation, an object in transition between one kind of being and another. This is why it is such a compelling starting point for a materialist analysis of media. The corpse is not merely an apt metaphor. Rather, its analysis leads to a new understanding of what constitutes mediation, here understood as the relationship between the objects and attachments of everyday life and the sphere of technological representation in which we are all increasingly active participants. Attending to the corpse as a thing opens up a theorization of the material substrate of communication—it holds "media" accountable to its all-too-often latent connotation of physical medium. But by choosing the corpse as a starting point and not, for example, technologies conventionally associated with media studies such as radio or television, the symbolic power that this object wields stands in sharp relief. In other words, there is no biological determinism possible with the corpse, for its physicality is also the reason for its cultural power. To begin with the corpse, itself a hybrid object, is to thus find a third way out of the long established tendency toward determinism in the field, be it technological, economic, or cultural determinism.

Technologies of inscription and archive are central to the modern encounter with the dead. Friedrich Kittler's remark quoted in the epigraph to this introduction reminds us of the reasons why media studies might want to account for the corpse. As our capacities to capture and transmit the real expand, we find ourselves with an ever-growing archive of dead (but animated) souls. But while Kittler goes on to annihilate the human, I look to death for a media theory inextricable from humanity. It is true that any time we watch a silent film or flip through a book of old photographs, we are entering the realm of the dead. But some parts of that realm are more clearly marked as graveyards than others. Some archival images are always already dead (or as Bazin might put it, they offer us "death every afternoon"[3]), for example, the CCTV images of Princess Diana exiting the hotel en route to her fatal automobile crash. Those are the areas of interest here, the images that, even inscribed from life, transmit to us a uniquely modern, embodied iconography of death. If we want to understand better the role media play in our lives, we could do worse than to look at how they help us make sense of death.

WHAT IS A CORPSE?

How does the body itself, as a thing in the world, interact with the image and with discourse? How does its materiality play a part in rituals of death and mourning and practices of disposal, burial, and preservation? What, if any, trace of that materiality is legible in the cultural and discursive processes of memorialization? Corpses are bodies without agency or subjectivity, but they are not reducible to signification: they are, in some indisputable way, "real," even without the agency we ascribe to subjectivity.

This complex intertwining of the discursive and the biological is why the corpse is such a rich site for exploring what we mean by materialism. The use of the term *materialism* in this book assumes that matter is neither inert, ineffable noumenon—the unreachable "thing in itself"—nor reducible to signification. The study of media is both conduit and substrate in this understanding of materiality.

So what is a corpse? A corpse may be said to be an assemblage of multiple elements, some of which are human and some of which are not. *Assemblage* as I understand it from Deleuze and Guattari's use of the term[4] indicates its nonhierararchical arrangement of elements and their shifting heterogeneity. The corpse is an excellent example of both. The flesh itself is taxonomically human, but because it is no longer living, it is not functionally human. It is also a particular molecular and chemical combination, and these are in constant flux both in the living organism and after it has died. Then there are the bacteria that undertake the process of decomposition and the conditions (temperature, moisture, acidity) under which they work.

There may also be introduced—by human agency—chemical detergents, resins, and waxes that slow this process of decomposition. A corpse may also be photographed, another technological intervention that captures the moments before decomposition. I will look at both of these interventions, embalming and photography, as part of the emergent effects of corpses as hybrid, nonhierarchical assemblages of technological, biological, and cultural elements. These technologies are important, but they interact or assemble with a thing that is already inherently communicative because it is referential.

The corpse is a special kind of thing in that it has a special relationship to subjectivity. That relationship is referential, or pointing; a corpse is, among other things, a gesture *toward*. To *refer* comes from the Latin "to bear or carry"—to carry again, to bring something to something else again. To *refer* also entails a gesture of intention, as in the pointed finger or the arrow. Finally, reference is a grammatical structure, a kind of linguistic shorthand, as for example in pronouns, which must always have a specific antecedent, a clear reference to a specific noun (which is, of course, a kind of thing). If reference saturates our language and our gestures, it is because its ineffable movement sits on the threshold of life and death—the place where culture makes meaning of an otherwise brutish world.

As "remains," the corpse is a referential thing—it is the remains *of someone*. Even when that someone is not identified, a corpse always references a human departure, a specific subject who has left it behind. Often this reference happens by means of physical resemblance: the first recourse in identifying a corpse is visual recognition, and only later are measures taken that are not explicitly visual, such as dental records or DNA testing. As organic material, however, the corpse precisely differs from its antecedent, the deceased. The deceased is what is "no longer with us." The corpse's materiality is thus also the site of its difference from the deceased, and from the memory of the deceased, and hence the site of its polysemy. In the flesh—precisely where embalming and photography make their different interventions—the corpse differs as much as it resembles. This hybridity points toward the heterogeneity of legacy in that someone's memory is made of discursive elements but her corpse, as a different element in that legacy, may always undermine or change the discourse.

Finally, the corpse is a liminal thing. The referential relationship to subjectivity that makes it special is a fleeting one: as soon as decomposition begins, the corpse looks less and less like the deceased and becomes more and more a site of horror and abjection.[5] Its ontology is unstable, its resemblance fleeting, its power to refer bounded by time and by the material constraints of the biological flesh itself.

CORPUS: THE BODY OF THE NATION, MARTYRED BODIES, TABLOID BODIES

Iconography is a specifically visual practice, so when we talk about an iconography of the flesh, we are specifically asking about how the visual (linked here particularly with embalming and photography) works to determine our notions of the corpse. Paradoxically enough, corpses become meaningful as matter through the visual, particularly because of the visual bias of contemporary funeral practices (see later for a more detailed analysis of this bias). The analysis of the book thus depends on careful attention to the way the corpse as matter interacts with the visual.

The book is organized by chapters to highlight three major themes of how the corpse works via the visual, both to figure mediation and as a literal medium. These are "The Body of the Nation" (chapter 1), "Martyred Bodies" (chapter 2), and "Tabloid Bodies" (chapter 3). Each chapter thematizes the corpse as a relation between the visual (iconography) and the material (the flesh). Starting with the medieval metaphor of the nation as a body with the king as its head, I move on to the martyred bodies of Emmett Till, whose 1955 lynching helped spark the American civil rights movement, and Hamza al-Khateeb, a Syrian boy whose mutilated corpse showed the world the brutality of the Assad regime via a YouTube video. Their stories are known because their mutilated bodies testify to injustice, suffering, and brutality. In life, they were ordinary people—children—but in death they become points of identification for a group of people otherwise marginalized and dispossessed. Tabloid bodies are the opposite—bodies that in life are an equal focus of scrutiny, scandal, and adoration and whose untimely deaths are media events in which the moral importance of their deaths is constructed via a complex negotiation of their relationship with the image. In contrast to the martyred body, the tabloid body becomes a martyr to fame only in its invisible characteristics, in an unseen essence that transcends the intense visibility of a tabloid life.

I identify each corpus according to its embodied characteristic: as the body of the nation, the body of the martyr, and the body of tabloid celebrity. This book specifically works on what I'll call *iconic corpses*—corpses of people (some public figures, others figures made public in death) whose deaths occasion public narratives about the nation, suffering, the other. The legacies of the iconic dead touch on key notions of identity, ethics, and politics.

The corpses analyzed in detail here are not meant to compose an exhaustive list of iconic corpses nor even to be representative of particular strategies. I've chosen them because they left a corpus, an archive of public and mediated mourning. Though Michael Jackson was perhaps not universally mourned, his death occasioned public displays of grief, as did those of Princess Diana and Eva Perón. The figures in this book also count as "iconic corpses" because their lives are defined by death, their stories inseparable from their endings. As much as Evita, Diana, or Michael Jackson did in life, their deaths dominate the stories of their lives. They are always already dead, in the public imagination—martyrs to causes or targets of prejudice or tragic victims of their own failings.

Hamza al-Khateeb and Emmett Till, conversely, are ordinary people elevated to the status of public figures because of their untimely, brutal, and ultimately politically charged deaths. In this sense, their deaths are incidents of mourning where the loss is felt differently; as we will see, both deaths are tied to political causes, where each boy becomes a point of identification. Most of us mourn Emmett Till not because we knew him but because he might have been someone we knew, and because he died because of hatred and injustice. The ways in which the boys' bodies become part of this kind of mourning is crucial here.

The nation is a long-standing corporeal metaphor, bringing together physical space and geographical boundaries with the heterogeneous and sometimes diasporic notion of a people. Issues of ethnic belonging, of shared values, cultural and linguistic practices, and history, are all negotiated through the rhetoric and iconography of the nation. The body of the king is often metaphorically linked to the body of the nation, via what Kantorowicz designated as the "king's two bodies."[6] Chapter 1 begins with Abraham Lincoln's corpse, a kind of threshold case between the Victorian cult of death and the modern impulse to rationalize and exclude death from the productive center of life. Though not precisely kings, Vladimir Lenin and Eva Perón were both embalmed and displayed as icons of the nation, thus making these "two bodies" a literal emblem. Their embalmed bodies became important sites of contestation about what the history, boundaries, and future of the nation should be.

In the corpses of Evita and Lenin, there is an indexical or causal relationship between the body as matter and the figurative body of the nation. The literalism of indexicality—its power to "bear away our faith"[7]—in this corpus uses embalming as the technology suturing the iconography to the corpse as matter. Lenin's tomb, where his embalmed corpse has been displayed since his death, is thus perhaps one of the most visible icons of the body of the nation. The relative stability of Lenin's entombment gives the impression that his body is eternal and its iconography unchanging. To help illustrate the ways in which even a long-term display like Lenin's is itself unstable because of the liminal nature of the corpse, I turn to the body of Eva Perón. Perón was also embalmed for display, but the political conditions in Argentina resulted in the military appropriating and concealing her body for nearly twenty years, ultimately burying it in Europe under a false name. During this absence, Perón's supporters used the curious case of the body as a tool in their ongoing quest to regain political power. The military finally returned the body to Argentina in 1974, when it was buried in a tomb in the Recoleta Cemetery. Though the preserved body cannot be seen, thousands of tourists and local pilgrims visit the tomb in Buenos Aires every year.

The case of the body of Eva Perón is fantastic. Its various custodians, mostly military men, suffered all kinds of misfortunes that led to the mythology of a curse on the body. Because Perón was a woman and her body was highly (and ambiguously) sexualized in life, the story of her corpse also includes claims of necrophilia and mutilation. My main point of entry into this story is the documentary *The Unquiet Grave,* made by Peronist sympathizers and aired on Argentine public television in 1997, which dramatizes the body's turbulent fifty-year history. Its focus is on the claim that the corpse was brutally mutilated by the military, a claim it purports to prove by showing hitherto unseen photographs of the damaged corpse at the time of its exhumation and subsequent reburial in the early 1970s. In its dependence on these shocking photographs, *The Unquiet Grave* reinforces the indexicality of the embalming and the photograph as well as the related indexicality of the damage to the corpse itself, which points toward the violence of its custodians. The documentary thus constructs a particular legacy for the body of Eva Perón in which her vulnerable corpse is first abused, then rescued, in both cases by men.

I read *The Unquiet Grave* as an opportunity to attend to the corpse as a material site of heterogeneity. Against the airtight case the (leftist, Peronist) filmmakers seek to construct against the (right-wing, anti-Peronist) military, there emerges the uncontainable and irreducible heterogeneity of this body, whose politics, gender identification, and ongoing legacy are anything but stable. In particular, other elements in the corpus of Eva Perón tend to "queer" the body, making its sexuality subversive and, by extension, questioning the homonormativity of the nation it represents.

The sexual difference and queerness in the example of the body of Eva Perón as the body of the nation illustrates the ways in which the physical body becomes a site for contested meaning. The martyred bodies discussed in chapter 2 illustrate the ways in which the corpse is called on to index injustice via graphic depiction. Here the image becomes a conduit to the body as its own index of suffering: the wounds depicted point toward an unspeakable brutality to which this now-mute flesh bears silent witness.

This chapter and the following chapter explore the politics of whose body must be visible in death and suffering and whose bodily suffering and death may be kept invisible. In the case of corpuses where a dead body is an "anyone" whose legacy is an ethical statement about race (or about human rights and distant suffering), the corpse must function visually. In contrast to the indexical functioning of the photographic or embalmed corpse that worked to maintain a particular identity, however, these corpses rely on both photographic indexicality and metaphorical tension to construct a corpus that casts the body as an "anyone" of imaginary identification: your son, your brother, you.

How are corpses read as an injunction to remember that is tied to the struggle for political recognition of certain ethnic groups? Here the power to be seen—to be recognized, to be politically visible—is also articulated to the right to control the conditions under which one is seen. In this corpus, the visibility of the corpse—whether its materiality must be visually marked or is presented as irreducible to visual representation—also indexes cultural values about whose identity is unique and whose is meant to be "representative" of a particular ethnic group and its struggles for political recognition. The "matter" of the 1955 lynching of thirteen-year-old Emmett Till is in his flesh as visible artifact. Till's mother deliberately allowed *Jet* magazine to publish photographs of the open-casket funeral, confronting readers with visual evidence of the savage brutality of his death. Today this image is available in any number of contexts online and in print, with historical context or without. Till's story as a person is not really available beyond a few biographical details centered around the circumstances of his death, such as his age at the time, whom he was visiting, and where he grew up. The only images of Till in life are visual "gravestones," images of a boy marked for death. There is no life story, only a story of death.

Bodily suffering is unspeakable in that it is unimaginable in its horror, and yet it calls on us with terrible urgency to somehow bear witness.[8] Throughout the history of visual culture in the West, images have been used to call for an ethical response to the suffering of distant others.[9] Images of dead and mutilated bodies are central to this history, but the focus here is on particular bodies, bodies that refer (at least in part) to a specific person. The examples discussed in chapter 2 illustrate how the body acts as a call to attend to others by struggling to depict the embodied horrors of physical suffering. Unlike photographs of anonymous victims of atrocity, the dead bodies considered here call on us in the name of a particular someone. Again, however, there is an important distinction between "someone" and "someone as anyone." These are martyred bodies, bodies primarily defined by their witnessing.

The mutilated corpse of the Syrian boy Hamza al-Khateeb is the martyred body at the center of a humanitarian plea to the West. His body is taken up in a political cause by means of visualization: a video taken of his mutilated and castrated corpse and a Facebook page, "We Are ALL Hamza Al-khateeb," that displays other photographs of dead and mutilated children in his name to call the world to responsibility in the Syrian conflict. The power and the pathos of this call depend on the vulnerability of his naked, mutilated corpse being shown to the world, in particular to a world of Western observers to whom his life and death would be utterly foreign. In this sense, al-Khateeb's body is itself the iconography of suffering and again a literal emblem of one reading of nation, its identity indistinguishable from its death. The *corpus* of Hamza al-Khateeb deploys the indexicality of the video (and of the wounds inflicted on the body that the video shows) to articulate this suffering body to the suffering of a nation. Much like what we saw in *The Unquiet Grave,* indexicality is used to ensure that the body as physical thing is solidly connected to the abstract body of the nation: to literalize the suffering of Syria for an audience removed from the site. The ways in which this body's vulnerability must be used to communicate this idea to a Western audience are political in the sense that al-Khateeb's special personhood is subsumed under the weight of his visibility as victim and martyr.

The third corpus examines what I call tabloid bodies, bodies who are considered martyrs to fame. In life, their embodiment was a source of scandal and anxiety, but in death they are redeemed, and the scandal of their bodies is transformed into stigmata. In chapter 3, I look at the live funerals of the biggest tabloid celebrities of the 1980s and 1990s, Michael Jackson and Princess Diana. In death, both Diana and Michael Jackson were recast as martyrs to fame, figures who used their sometimes scandalous visibility to raise awareness of the plight of others. This reimagining of their tabloid celebrity allows their media archive to retain its value: Diana's death redeems the British monarch as a consumer object, as Michael Jackson's death sells records and films. These tabloid bodies are abject in death, expelled from the otherwise highly visible archive of their lives.[10] That we cannot see them as corpses indicates to what degree the dead have been expelled from modern life and the ways in which our communication with the dead has been reduced to a one-sided dialogue. Tabloid bodies illustrate all we are missing in our communication with the dead, which requires not so much an archive of endlessly repeatable images as a willingness to enter into a radically asymmetrical dialogue with the dead, one that cannot be reduced to the neutral third term of exchange.

Jackson's corpus tends to deemphasize the visual record to construct his legacy in the United States as a key cultural figure in the civil rights movement. Using footage from the live televised memorial, I show that the fact that Jackson did not, at the time of his death, "look black" is problematic for the construction of Jackson's legacy as an African American. This problem is "managed" by putting the political focus on the casket, which prominently appears in the memorial. In this way, the "truth" of Jackson's contributions to racial equality in the United States, particularly as articulated by the eulogy of the Reverend Al Sharpton, is located in the unseen material fact of his dead body and not in the visual archive of his very public life.

According to Sharpton's rhetoric, Jackson's body, so controversial in life, in death became a conduit for other bodies of color, his essential blackness allowing for the public appearance of other black bodies, such as Barack Obama.[11] Princess Diana's body, also controversial and profligate in life, has been eulogized as an ideal medium, a telegraph transmitting distant suffering via her own misfortunes. In death, however, there are no images of her suffering—these images indeed exist but have been suppressed by the British monarchy and legal system. Diana's corpus includes only photographs taken in life. In this sense, the loss of Diana is felt as a sort of closing of that special conduit of empathy. There is a sense in which this legacy is handed down to her children, and for this aspect of the legacy to function, the ongoing profitability of the monarchy as a tourist attraction and celebrity industry must be ensured. Allowing Diana's body invisibility in its suffering and to function simply as the radiant and youthful medium of the suffering of others points to the politics of how bodies are called on to mean in death.

The themes of nation, martyrdom, and otherness are addressed via corpses that are iconic[12] in the sense that they are proper, particular. They are taken *of someone,* that is, they are not anonymous victims of a disaster or disappeared bodies of political dissidents or terrorism victims. There exists a substantial and authoritative literature on these kinds of images of death, most notably Barbie Zelizer's recent work.[13] In contrast, my interest here is in bodies whose subjectivity is not "mass" but "proper"—as in a proper name. These deaths are not anonymous but particular, not only because they are singular (one person) but because that one person had been afforded the particularly modern sense of a "name," of "being somebody."

Representations—images, texts, embalmings, memorials, relics—all work to establish (however contingently) a particular relationship to the material that an iconic corpse embodies. Even images of the iconic dead in life become images of someone haunted by the historical fact of death, which is now known to contemporary consumers of the image. When, for example, Argentine president Cristina Kirchner selects a photographic portrait of Eva Perón as the basis for a building-high mural, she not only posits a particular relationship to the persona of Evita (which is of course her explicit political aim) but also, in its iconicity,[14] figures the relationship between Evita the global pop culture artifact and Evita the particularly Argentine political inheritance. It comments on what permanence is and what of the body may not be represented. This representation of iconic death is thus a figuring, a metaphorical positing of the relationship between the very real, very dead body of Eva Perón and its power to signify beyond itself.

The book concludes with a reexamination of the politics of legacy now that the corpse has been reintroduced as an actant in any given "corpus." In this light, the modern taboo of death (and what Gorer calls its resultant pornographic obsession)[15] appears as an effort to fix identity via a visual media archive that itself effaces the physicality of the corpse. I argue that it is crucial to attend to the particular ways the corpse means as matter because it is in the corpse that difference and diversity reside, as well as the flux of time and change. In this space of uncertainty, any attempt to memorialize or create legacy is not only inevitable but also a strategic gesture, one that reveals much of our ideological investments in the iconography of death. In particular, this iconography serves to monetize the corpse and make it productive in a post-Fordist economy where images and archival media may continue to produce economic value long after the living body has deceased. In examples of deaths whose iconography is not specifically commodified—that is, in cases where the corpus articulates to ethical ideals of social justice and civil rights—we see a heightened visibility of the corpse that makes the death, and not a celebration of life, the center of the corpus. As these ethical appeals move into the highly monetized and commodified space of social and digital media, the deaths themselves become commodified. Images of the deceased become pornographic in the sense of excessively, unbearably visible. To attend to the corpse as the site of any number of other stories besides those told in the received legacies of these iconic deaths is thus to rescue the dignity and the polysemy of their lives and to honor the diverse ways and reasons that these lives are mourned.

The received legacies are the result of Western mourning and mortuary practices that privilege the visual in particular and contingent ways. To understand how specific these practices are to the examples that we'll encounter in the book, I provide a brief analysis of funeral practices in the West, where, as Baudrillard asserts, the dead are mainly characterized by their expulsion from symbolic exchange with the living.[16] In particular, these practices privilege the visual aspect of the dead: death as image and representation.

MORTUARY RITUALS, PHOTOGRAPHY, AND EMBALMING

Mortuary Rituals

Mourning and disposal rituals are one of the few cultural universals. All cultures develop practices to mark the social significance of the transition from life to death.[17] This universality nevertheless embraces immense variation in the specific details of how death is understood, observed, and mourned and how dead bodies are disposed. The body of the corpse is thus the site of a crucial intersection between the particularity of culture and the universality of death as a biological and material reality. The corpses examined in this book are contingent expressions of a cultural and historical moment *as well as* biological, material entities.

Several themes emerge from the sociological and anthropological literature on death, mourning, and disposal that help contextualize the particularly Western, industrial practices of photography and embalming. Specifically, embalming and photography both privilege the visual in their intervention in the body of the deceased. This means that contemporary mortuary rituals perform the universal functions of separation of the living from the dead, marking of social status, and marking the transformation from corpse to memory by means of a visual rhetoric that is itself not universal but particular to our cultural and historical formation. Each example analyzed in the following chapters is therefore iconographic in this particular sense—as an image of memory in shifting relationship to the corpse that is the physical referent of that memory. This material body signifies in relationship to this iconography in varying ways that illustrate what precisely is at stake in constructions of legacy with regard to embodied ideals like race, class, gender, and bodily suffering. Legacies are memories with an instructive or prescriptive edge: the bodies that anchor their iconographies are very real sites of difference in whose name the iconography urges us to ethical action.

All mortuary rituals work to separate the body of the dead from the realm of the living and to escort it on its journey from physical artifact to socially enshrined memory or legacy. Different cultures may bury their dead, mummify them, cremate them, or even, as in the case of some Amazonian cultures, ritually consume them.[18] In each case, however, the idea is to physically transform the flesh from the decomposing corpse of the deceased into a ritual object that may then take its place in social memory by means of a gravestone, burial site, or other form of disposal. The site of social memory is underpinned by beliefs about an eternal spirit or soul, which is also a social universal. Members of the Cheyenne tribe believe that the dead visit the living in dreams to offer advice;[19] the Wari people literally incorporate the spirit of the dead by consuming their flesh;[20] the "disappeared" spirits of those tortured and murdered during the period of state terror in Argentina retained political agency after death as their missing bodies were recovered and reburied and human rights activism undertaken in their names.[21] In each case these rituals work to restore the social cohesion that death by necessity disrupts, though as the last example illustrates, this cohesion may be a contested and hard-won reality rather than a smooth, traditionally mediated transition.

Western attitudes toward and rituals surrounding death have undergone several important shifts. These were periodized by the French historian Philippe Ariès in *The Hour of Our Death*,[22] which is still considered the definitive history of Western European death attitudes and practices. Ariès identifies four themes whose shifting importance has led to five different death models over the past millennium: (1) the sense of the individual, (2) the defense of society against the unpredictable forces of nature, (3) a belief in life after death, and (4) a belief in the existence of evil. As the sense of the individual, for example, rises in importance in the course of Western European culture, the death model shifts. Death is no longer a nonpersonal, social event but concerns the individual soul and the grief and separation of loved ones. As belief in the eternal soul and evil fade in the modern period, death models place less emphasis on the role of the soul in the afterlife and more on the fear of death as isolation and social nonexistence. In Ariès's taxonomy, death for modern Western culture is "remote and imminent," a continual threat to the self that cannot be appeased or understood in its radical alterity. Modern death also follows a "death of the other" model in that the fear of death is not focused one's own death (a fear that is presumably repressed or considered irrelevant given the nihilism of secular society) but on the grief that accompanies the loss of loved ones.

This Western history of mortuary practice and attitudes toward death is the context in which we must consider the practices of embalming and photography, because they developed in a time when the concept of the individual was highly developed and valued and the fear of separation from loved ones was a central concern. Both of these practices are used in modern mortuary rituals to preserve the individual's social role in memory by means of a particularly visual modality.

The technologies of photography and embalming play a crucial but not identical role to create a meaningful legacy when someone dies. Embalming developed after the practice of postmortem photography was well established and adopted its aesthetic of death as a visual exhibition of peaceful sleep. Moreover, the chemical and mechanical innovations of embalming create what John Troyer calls the "postmortem condition,"[23] that is, a corpse that, like modern media, manipulates space and time in particular ways that lead to important shifts in its commodification and legal status. The mobility and visibility of the modern corpse are the direct result of embalming technology, which allowed a preserved corpse to be transported long distances without significant visible disintegration. This innovation, formerly available only through representation with postmortem photography, deeply informs our contemporary relationship with the corpse. Specifically, the historical intertwining of the roots of photography and embalming does much to explain the complex role of visual media in what I am calling the "corpus" or media assemblage of any given death. Following Deleuze and Guattari, I am theorizing a corpus as a nonhierarchical assemblage of biological, physical, cultural, and discursive objects with dynamic and emergent effects. For this reason, a particular element, such as photography, may work differently in the different examples discussed in each corpus. A corpus involves the physical body of the deceased, but it also organizes images of that body in life and sometimes in death, texts that construct the legacy of the deceased person, as well as technologies, such as photography and embalming, that allow the corpse to circulate as a communicative object. The Latin word *corpus* refers either to a physical body or a figurative one, as in a body of literature or facts or ideas. My use of the word is thus intended to invoke the complex and dynamic relationship between the corpse as a physical object and the discursive strategies and media technologies that make it meaningful as matter.

Photography and Embalming

André Bazin famously remarked that "the photograph embalms time,"[24] occasioning an entire body of scholarship on the relationship between the photographic image, indexicality, and death.[25] Photography is not only like embalming, however—embalming is like photography. Both technologies developed in the context of a "larger, emergent culture of preservation" in the nineteenth century.[26] These media not only preserved the liminal, representational quality of corpses but also shaped the look of the modern corpse.[27] These practices thus came to delineate and police how bodies became meaningfully "legible" representations of death and its relationship to representation.

Photography and embalming are both media that seek to capture and forestall the corpse's inherent liminality. Photography does this by capturing the image of the corpse before it rots; embalming does it by intervening chemically in the process of putrefaction itself. Despite their different techniques, both mediations preserve the appearance of the flesh as such. The embalmed corpse, like the subject of postmortem photography before it, looks "as if it were sleeping," suspended between this life and the next.

Mediation of death via photography and embalming is also congruent with the effacement of death from modern life, making the corpse's legibility—the conditions under which it may or may not meaningfully appear as legacy, memory, reference to a deceased—not only an historical question but also an ideological one.

As a result, with industrialization and urbanization—central movements in both the history of media and of the subject—the corpse is uniquely positioned in mass society as both "deceased subject" and commodity (object). Indeed, as embalmers became experts who had to be licensed and regulated, they began to be active and paid participants in private experiences of mourning. One has only to think of the quiet space of the funeral home viewing room and the laboratories hidden beneath to grasp the complex boundaries modern embalming maintains between public and private, science and nature.

I also see a crucial parallel between the wet mount emulsions that would democratize photography and the chemical solution that made the corpse a "postmortem subject." Embalming is of interest not only as a technology—the pump—but also because the fluid is a chemical used to preserve the flesh in the appearance of life. For both media, this chemical inscription becomes the technological grounding of an ideological truism: the corpse's univocal reference to the deceased.

As photographs of the dead entered into the collection of artifacts and relics used in the cultural representation of grief and death, so too did ideas about how a dead body should look and be looked at. Generally, the corpse as we know it today may be said to have emerged out of what Crary has called the "disciplining of vision" in the nineteenth century.[28] More specifically, the relationship between postmortem photography and embalming outlined here supports Gunning's assertion that nineteenth-century photography produced the "standardization of imagery" for industrial societies.[29] As photography established how to make visible the conditions of life under industrialization and modernity, it also provided a template to envision death under the same.

Photography predates embalming technology by about thirty years, and it wasn't until about 1890 that embalming became widespread enough to replace ice as the dominant form of preservation.[30] Embalming inherited a certain "look" for the corpse that portraiture and death photography had established, making its preservative goals not merely literal (stopping decomposition) but also symbolic, in the sense that the corpse signifies peaceful sleep. The practice of postmortem photography informed the aesthetics of embalming, the ways it represents death in the medium of the flesh.

This aesthetic represents death as peace, and as ultimately conserving the social identity of the deceased. People die in all kinds of confusion, agony, and bodily distortion. Funeral convention demands that we erase these signs of suffering from the countenance of the deceased. Just as embalming protects us, as Quigley writes, from the "sights, sounds and smells"[31] of our loved one's impending putrefaction, so does the arrangement of the body protect us from imagining her suffering. It places the body in a kind of future perfect, when the deceased will have been received happily into the fold of whatever afterlife awaits, at peace with her life and with those she left behind. Embalming and postmortem photography create an image of what we imagine the experience of death to be like, the "as if" of modern, mediated death—not the past reality to which the facial expression and body position may seem to refer but an imagined place beyond.[32] Because they use the body and the likeness of the deceased as the medium of this representation, embalming and photography, read as elements in assemblages, produce the effect of a stable identity that will persevere in memory even as the physical remains disappear.

Before the advent of photography, families with substantial means often commissioned deathbed portraits or death masks. Paintings had to be undertaken very quickly but, like most portraits, were not necessarily prized for their realism.[33] Mourning portraits might depict living members of a family alongside the deceased, whose death was indicated only symbolically (a weeping willow in the background, a stopped watch, etc.). Death masks satisfied the indexical urge to capture exactly the features of the deceased, though they were always taken after minimal composition of the features (eyes and mouth closed).[34] These practices, however, were limited to those with extensive means (or great renown) and were thus not widespread. Photography took over and democratized these practices, as well as providing a new, more faithfully iconic way of capturing the corpse in the short time before decay eats away at its resemblance to the deceased (or to anything living).

From about 1840 to 1890, before the widespread adoption of embalming, photographers could count on a steady income in funeral portraits. Moreover, professional photographers explicitly advertised that their services included portraits of deceased persons.[35] A family with neither the means nor the inclination for living likenesses might hire a photographer in the case of a death. Often these images were the only likenesses ever taken of the person (especially, but not only, if the deceased was a child). Moreover, corpses made much more compliant subjects than the living, whose stern, cramped expressions were often the result of having to hold uncomfortably still to accommodate long exposure times. Corpses were photographed at home immediately postmortem as a unique way of preserving the appearance of the deceased. For this reason, the focus is on the deceased's face and head, the close-up providing not just a memento but also a faithful likeness.[36]

In privileging iconic reference to the deceased, the practices of postmortem photography also developed a visual rhetoric about death in the medium of the flesh. Platitudes about the "pencil of nature" notwithstanding, corpse photographers did more than simply record likeness: they also created a portrait of death as peaceful sleep.[37] They might use mirrors or other reflective surfaces to accommodate lighting difficulties and performed simple postmortem adjustments, such as rotating eyeballs in their sockets using the "handle of a teaspoon."[38] Funeral photographer Josiah Southworth describes some of the tricks of his trade, assuring his fellow photographers that in the moments immediately following death, bodies are meek and pliable: "Just lay them down as if they were in a sleep. . . . Then place your camera and take your pictures just as they would look in life."[39] In this way, postmortem photographers used the corpse as the medium to represent ideas about death in general even as they worked to capture the likeness (and thereby secure the social memory) of an individual person.

Photography is thus a key player in the construction of the modern corpse. Postmortem photographs become different kinds of documents once other techniques of preservation are available to "secure the shadow" in a different manner. After the advent of embalming, postmortem photographs were more likely to use special techniques to create a likeness that appeared to be not just asleep but actually alive. The negative might be rotated to give the appearance that a supine corpse was actually seated upright, or the negative might be painted to make it look as if the eyes were open. Here the appearance of life, and not just death as peaceful sleep, becomes for a time the special provenance of the photograph. As the funeral industry expanded, postmortem photographs increasingly recorded not only the deceased but the mise-en-scène of the funeral parlor, with its ornate caskets and wreaths, and often with the mourners posed around the casket. In these images, the corpse itself is very small, and it is not its likeness, but rather the event of the funeral itself, that is being recorded.[40]

Embalming takes over for photography the task of preserving the identity of the deceased in the medium of the flesh, at least for the period of time before the body is buried. Much like photography, then, embalming may be read as a media practice, that is, as an intervention that allows manipulations in space and time. Embalming conforms to a particular *image* of death first standardized in postmortem photography.[41] Posed photographs of corpses produced an appearance of life that standardized how corpses would be called on to refer to and memorialize the departed. These photographic conventions would later help determine the embalmed corpse's social role, especially as these images began to circulate as commodities (cartes de visite, commissioned portraits, etc.).

Modern embalming was invented in France by Jean-Nicolas Gannal, whose "special process," patented in 1837, arrested tissue decay via an injection of solution of aluminum sulfate. Sometimes called chemical or mechanical embalming, this procedure lengthened the time a corpse could remain open to the air without decomposition. In so doing, it also permitted the corpse to travel home for burial and arrive still recognizable as the deceased. In their *History of American Funeral Directing*, Robert Habenstein and William Lamers locate the Civil War as the first widespread instance of mechanical embalming in the United States, with "embalmers waiting and working in camps, on battlefields, in government hospitals, and in nearby railroad centers."[42]

Previous to the use of modern embalming technologies, if corpses were preserved at all, it was for very brief periods, either using some kind of ice-based refrigeration or (in the absence of ice) submersion in a cold creek. Burial happened almost immediately, and near the place of death—whether or not this was home (war dead were often buried or burned on or near battlefields, for example). In the rare occasion of an attempt to transport a corpse by rail, an airtight metal casket was used. These containers were meant only to transport remains, not preserve them; moreover, they were unreliable even in this aspect, as they sometimes exploded under the pressure of the gases released by the decomposing corpse.[43]

Unlike other forms of preservation, embalming allowed the body to retain a stable and recognizable reference to the appearance of the deceased for longer periods of time. Ice preservation, for example, does not slow decomposition enough to allow for more than limited transport or display—and before modern refrigeration, it was at best messy and expensive and more likely impossible. Freezing the body, rather than simply keeping it cool, allows for preservation of the flesh but irrevocably destroys delicate tissues. Corpses that were frozen during the winter and awaited a spring burial, once thawed, bore no resemblance to the deceased, and indeed presented a grotesque and troubling appearance. Embalming is chemical, not physical, and although it radically alters the chemical composition of tissues,[44] it actually preserves appearances according to a photographic notion of fidelity.

The mechanics of chemical or mechanical embalming are relatively simple. The basic innovation is a handheld vacuum pump (now electric) that injects the dead body with a preservative chemical solution using the circulatory system. The organic bodily fluids are first drained, also using the vacuum pump, thus minimizing the embalmer's invasion into the body.[45] No internal organs are removed or preserved separately, because modern embalming uses already existing corporeal routes and processes (the circulatory system, osmosis) to radically alter the chemical composition of all bodily tissues via the introduction of embalming fluid.

Embalming fluid is a suspension of alcohols, resins, and waxes, along with detergents and disinfectants, that pervade the tissues via osmosis. Embalmings intended for permanent display, such as performed for Lenin and Evita, also involve the injection of fluids and dyes into skin around the mouth and eyes to prevent the disintegration or desiccation of this delicate tissue, as well as pliable rubber or plastic coatings for the body. The funeral director's art may now involve a detailed range of manipulations, tools, and cosmetics, even including surgeries in some cases. Kennedy, for example, was prepared for public viewing even though in the end the casket remained closed. Because of the massive damage to his head and face, a team of postmortem cosmetic surgeons faced the enormous task of making his corpse not only presentable but recognizable. In an illustrative mingling of the entertainment and funerary industries, so-called mortician's wax, which is used to rebuild crushed or torn facial tissues, was in the pre-computer-generated-imagery period also a key tool for the creation of special effects in film and television.

Given the dramatic changes it introduced in funerary practices, it is remarkable how quickly embalming was naturalized as part of the cultural process of death. Instead of merely washing the body while it rested on a board suspended over buckets of ice, families could bring the body to the funeral parlor, where a technician would embalm and prepare it for burial under laboratory-like conditions. When chemical embalming was still a relatively new technology, some feared that because of this intrusion, the embalmed dead would not be allowed into heaven.[46] Nevertheless, within a generation, embalming was standard practice. Jean-Nicolas Gannal's embalming manual was translated from French into English in 1840; between 1856 and 1869, eleven major patents were granted for fluids and processes, thus indicating a less than thirty-year span in which Gannal's "new process" was put to use and commodified.[47]

Thus embalming's early appeal was not so much in its power of preservation as in its power to preserve the appearance of life. An embalming ad from 1863 describes its service as "to admit of contemplation of the person Embalmed, with the *countenance* of one asleep."[48] *Countenance,* a rather antiquated term, refers particularly to the face as an indication of mood or expression. It highlights the face's expressive, communicative function. In other words, the face is to be "read" as indicating peaceful slumber, thus reinforcing Victorian attitudes toward death as the "long sleep" that were also the rhetoric of postmortem photography. This signifying countenance, in both media, constitutes legibility not only as a deceased person but also as a commentary on the way of all flesh.

Embalming introduces changes similar to the changes introduced by mass communication media with regard to the manipulation of space and time. For example, the embalmed corpse "circulated outside of conventional time and space," whereas before embalming, a kind of "corpse time" had determined practices surrounding mourning and burial.[49] A manipulation in time—the embalming—therefore also allows a manipulation of space.

Thus embalming not only emerged alongside major media, such as sound recording, photography, the railroad (known to the nineteenth century as "steam communication"), and the telegraph; it also shares in their narrative of technological domination over space and time. Human intervention in "corpse time" also allowed for physical transport of bodies. A preserved body, because it endures in time, is also much more easily transported in space, thus giving embalming technology a two-pronged domination and control over the "natural" corpse.[50] Insofar as chemical embalming privileges vision and allows for more control over the body in space and time, it partakes in many of the social changes wrought by an emerging mass media.

The embalmed corpse also exhibits the blurring between subject and object that characterizes the age of modern media.[51] As "postmortem subject" and commodified object, the corpse disrupts stable dualities between subjectivity and objecthood. It may be read as a special object whose last remnants of subjectivity—the embalming that allows it to meaningfully reference the deceased—confer on it a kind of marginal subjectivity. Nevertheless, it is in its status as object that it circulates as commodity, either within the economic system of the funeral industry or, as Lock shows, as the "field" from which organs are "harvested" and sold, gifted, or donated.[52] It is as thing—as flesh—that the embalmed corpse becomes a medium; it is on the flesh that embalming works and in the flesh that it presents itself as postmortem subject.

The modern corpse is therefore never a unitary, unmediated object but rather a dynamic collection of cultural, biological, and technological practices and processes. I call the assemblage of images, practices, processes, and texts surrounding the corpse a *corpus,* using the new materialist theory of the assemblage to analyze the corpse as the crucially vibrant origin of the different and often contrasting legacies.[53] To attend to the corpse in itself as just such a dynamic assemblage or polysemic corpus is to restore the material itself to a vital (if not strictly agentic) role. This restoration is particularly important because the hegemonic construction of the material is as inert or ineffable. This move toward stable (and thus more easily monetized) identity thus works to suppress difference and polysemy. In the case of the iconic deaths analyzed in this book, understanding the corpse as dynamic corpus thus acknowledges and helps give voice to nonhegemonic investments and interpretations of these figures and the political responsibility invoked by the iconography of their deaths.

A MATERIALIST THEORY OF MEDIA ACCOUNTS FOR ASYMMETRICAL RELATIONS WITH THE DEAD

A materialist media theory of the corpse gives a space to the body as the *site of difference* between the deceased and her legacy. It begins to describe what happens to a construct, such as race (or gender, or class), that is both discursive and embodied when that embodiment is stripped of its subjectivity—when it has both the elusive power and touching vulnerability of that most special of things, the corpse.

I use Deleuze and Guattari's notion of the assemblage, following Bennett's new materialist reading of the term, to theoretically attend to the corpse in its materiality as a site of difference and polysemy.[54] This is particularly important in the case of the iconic deaths analyzed here, because of "what happens" to race or to gender once a body is no longer a subject with agency. This is usually theorized from the point of view of cultural construction (from the outside) or of subjectivity. Can we dwell in the raced body, the gendered body, the body of the nation, the body of suffering—can we attend to these bodies, listen to them, when they no longer are able to speak to us in the language of subjectivity? To attend only to what other subjectivities make of them is to disregard the body itself as that site of difference, as the physical locus of what could be, of the stories not told or of contested and contrasting stories.

Corpses embody mediation without being wholly human, thus pointing us toward a materialist analysis of media. Photography and embalming are mediations that work on the corpse to produce an assemblage of meaningful grief, memory, and inheritance. When we apprehend the corpse as a culturally legible yet wholly material object, then, we deploy a rich variety of interpretive strategies to make sense of the material. Using assemblage theory allows us to account for nonhegemonic interpretations of the social value of any given deceased identity. Whenever a public figure dies, subsequent generations invoke and deploy his memory to legitimize actions and interpretations whose finality is never guaranteed. This memory has a material substrate, and it is this material substrate that makes real the possibility of polysemy and heterogeneity in memory and in the political action undertaken in its name.

1

THE BODY OF THE NATION

Abraham Lincoln, Vladimir Lenin, and Eva Perón

This chapter looks at how the dead body is called on to figure the "nation" as a privileged and proper enclosure. It presents three different corpses, examples of different configurations of the embalmed body and the photographic image. Corpses embalmed for display invest in a deeply naturalized indexical relationship between the embalming and the deceased. This relationship may be threatened by photographic indexicality because of its privileged relationship to the real. This capacity to "bear away our faith"[1] makes literal the corpse's representation of the body politic. This discussion begins a larger arc that describes the libidinal and capitalistic investments in the relationship between the corpse and the visual. Subsequent chapters explore the ways in which photographs alternately underpin and trouble how public figures are mourned and the ideals to which their legacies are ascribed.

The metaphor of the nation as corporation with the king as its head and the subjects as its members dates to the late Middle Ages.[2] Embalmings of heads of state make this figure literal by preserving the physical body of the leader as a symbol of the eternal body politic. The corpus "nation" is, in this sense, at once the most obviously representational and the most deeply naturalized. To embalm and display the dead leader is to make an overt representational claim about the continuity of the nation he represents—to literally re-present the body as figurative. At the same time, the physical relationship between the body and what it represents blurs the line between the literal and the figurative, thus naturalizing the indexical or causal relationship between the body and its embalming.

The bodies of nine world leaders have been embalmed for display: Soviet patriarchs Lenin and Stalin; fellow travelers Ho Chi Minh in Vietnam and Mao Zedong in China, and Kim Il-sung and Kim Jong-il of North Korea. Outside the Communist bloc, there is the Philippines's Ferdinand Marcos and, in South America, Eva Perón of Argentina and Hugo Chávez of Venezuela. Each of these was a charismatic leader powerfully identified with the people. Of these nine, only Evita and Stalin are buried; the rest are still maintained for public display.[3]

Corpses deployed in the field of the nation aim to make stable and hierarchical claims about which bodies count for inclusion, which ones "fit" the analogy forged between the corporeal and the corporation, and which ones don't. If representational thinking is also the mode in which the state reproduces itself,[4] this corpus describes deeply naturalized connections between the material body and the body politic—the "king's two bodies."[5] The figurative equation between the embalmed corpse and the nation works by analogy and negation: by sorting what is *like* from what is *not*. In a more lyrical tone, Carlos Fuentes writes that "the fatherland is impeccable and adamantine."[6] The corpse that figures the nation is similarly incorruptible and, by extension, eternal. The representational bond is forged between like qualities that are only intelligible, of course, in contrast to their implied negation—the proper corruption of the corpse is here suspended as it is called into the service of a powerful and ancient figure.

Contemporary practices surrounding death work to create a non-permeable border between the living and the dead.[7] The understanding of death as a threat to the sovereignty of the individual finds its analogue in the ways in which sovereign nations manage the death of a leader. One might wonder what falls outside such an enclosure. Like embalming, photography rescues the corpse from its "proper corruption." What is the metaphorical equivalent of this corruption? What threatens the nation with putrefaction, dissolution, and disappearance?

A dialogue with the dead might offer lessons from the perspective of universal history. A work of remembrance that enlists the voices of the departed might do more to keep their memories close. The dead call on our ethical action, which all too often we undertake in their name without proper thought or respect for the living. Like the living human body, corpses are "leaky"[8]—their boundaries more permeable, their enclosures less stable than the representational claims of these embalmed kings. Our task in this chapter will also be to identify places where these boundaries shimmer and shift, where forces within the assemblage of the corpse work to deterritorialize the nation.

I begin with a discussion of the display of Abraham Lincoln's corpse, because Lincoln's death highlights some interesting tensions between photography and embalming as indexical signs. A prohibition on photographing Lincoln's corpse creates a corpus in which the photograph functions less as an index than the embalming itself. Following Bazin's exploration of the photograph as an object with an independent ontology, I open up this particular moment as a way to show how the ontology of the photograph always threatens the reference to the deceased when it is not read as indexical, that is, as purely referential, but rather as an object independently able to reference multiple images, ideas, and affects. This problem will also occur with corpses that are displayed for generations, because they begin to function as independent objects with their own histories separate from the deceased to whom they are supposed to refer.

Such is the case of the corpse of Vladimir Lenin, the second example, which stays in one place and stubbornly endures. The duration of his corpse becomes the undoing of the original relationship between the body and the notion of permanent revolution, as circumstances change around the unchanging, unmoving body. In contrast, the nomadic afterlife of my third example, the embalmed corpse of Eva Perón, is a particularly rich source of these circumstantial deployments in which "other" nations and other histories are posited and just as quickly dismantled. These other relationships, despite or perhaps even because of their instability, point us toward ways in which the *matter* of the corpse—its material circumstances—works in very different ways than its representational relationships.

The examples discussed in this corpus do have a chronology, but the history sketched here should be understood as a contingent constellation, in the sense that first Benjamin and then Adorno give the term: a cluster of interrelated concepts and objects without a necessary link to a transcendent, linear historical narrative.[9] What I want to bring together here are changing moments in the relationship of the dead body to image and visibility, on one hand, and to time and duration, on the other. In the chapters that follow, we'll see that these relationships shift substantially, not only at later historical moments, but in different corpuses with different social, political, and affective circumstances.

LINCOLN'S CORPSE AT THE THRESHOLD OF MODERNITY

Lincoln's death coincided with the rise of chemical embalming in the United States, which, as we have seen, was used widely for the first time during the Civil War. Embalmed in arsenic, Lincoln's body traveled by train from Washington to Springfield, Illinois, and lay in state in Washington, Philadelphia, New York, Chicago, and Buffalo, as well as in the capitals of all seven states along the way. Mourners also gathered on the tracks to watch the Lincoln Special as it passed through 180 cities in seven states. In Chicago, the rate of mourners passing the casket was seven thousand an hour; in New York, five hundred thousand waited outside before the public was even admitted.[10]

Mourning Lincoln coincided for many with their grief over the millions of war dead and served also as a rededication of the reunited but still shaky nation. Thus Lincoln's embalmed body plays a central role in a secular hagiography wherein the fallen leader redeems the injured body of the nation.[11] Lincoln is a martyr whose death, as metaphorically linked to the suffering of the Civil War, cleansed the nation of the sin of slavery. Indeed, the Great Emancipator becomes a figure not only for the end of slavery but also for the cause of freedom against oppression in general.[12]

This was the context for the mourning of Lincoln, which took place on an unprecedented scale. Never before and never again would so many have such a direct experience of mourning an assassinated president.[13] Lincoln's death stretches the limits of nineteenth-century communication, reaching toward mass communication without all of the technologies that would later make this possible. Just thirty odd years after the telegraph and another forty or so away from the radio, Lincoln's death combines the protracted mourning of a Victorian wake with the new technologies of photography and embalming. Embalming allowed the corpse to travel and be viewed over a long period of time in several different places. It also likely contributed to the fact that Lincoln's body could still be visually identified when he was exhumed in 1901.[14] Later assassinations would have access to the technology to do such a wake but either lacked the popularity or, as with JFK, happened at a moment when mourning practices had changed to preclude the same kind of extended viewing of the corpse.[15]

Photography plays a complex role in the mourning of Lincoln's death. Lincoln was the first president to be extensively photographed. Photographic portraits of him give us, even now, a vivid sense of the detail of his features in a way that painted portraits never can. Specifically, facial flaws that would have otherwise been smoothed over by the portrait painter appear and become part of his iconography. The characteristic wart on his cheek, for example, appears in all its ordinary coarseness in photographs and, by extension, becomes a key visual cue in the myth of Lincoln as a homespun, ordinary man set on an extraordinary path.[16]

The body was photographed as it lay in state in New York, as those who gave permission did not know that Mrs. Lincoln had prohibited photographing the corpse. As we saw in the last chapter, this would not have been unusual for 1865, when postmortem photography was still common practice. Nevertheless, secretary of war Edwin Seward ordered the photographer's plates destroyed and all copies of the photograph seized.[17] The only copy that survived was the one kept by Seward himself and was not discovered until the 1950s in an archive in Springfield.[18] It was never published, though if you look at the photograph now and compare it to the engravings made of the New York lying in state, it is nearly identical—or even inferior—in its iconic fidelity. In other words, the public would have seen the image of Lincoln's lying in state, just not the *photographic* image.

Given that postmortem portraiture was widely practiced at the time, and the public had easy access to graphic descriptions and drawings of the body, what was the objection to the photograph? What might its suppression help us understand about the variously configured relationship between the body and the image at a moment—death—when that body's object quality is most anxiously felt? How did this image seem to threaten or undermine the desire to make meaning out of that matter?

The Lincoln death photograph is a window onto a moment rather

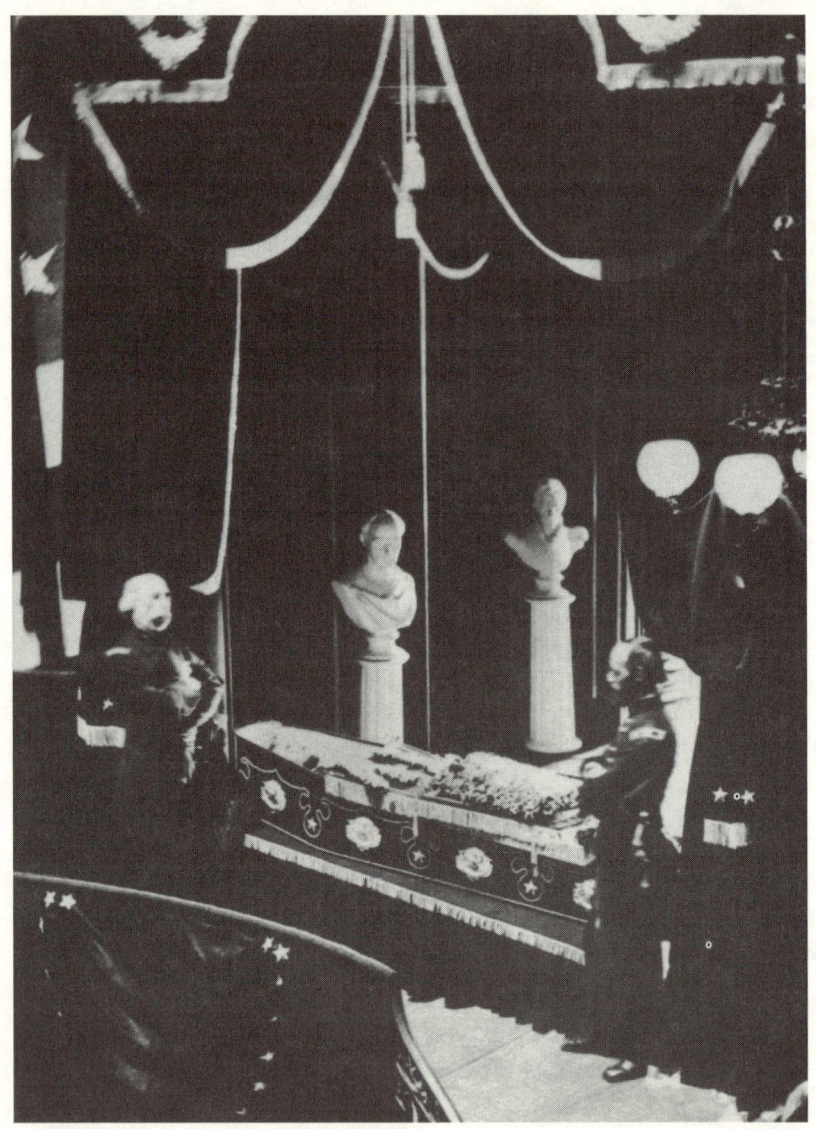

FIGURE I. Only surviving photograph of Lincoln's body lying in state, taken by Jeremiah Gurney. On Secretary Seward's order, all copies and plates of the photograph were to have been destroyed; this copy, apparently saved by Seward himself, was not discovered until 1952. Keya Morgan Collection, http://www.LincolnImages.com/.

FIGURE 2. A sketch that appeared in the May 6 issue Harper's Weekly shows the lying in state with more detail and "realism" than the photograph itself, suggesting that not the image itself, but rather its process of becoming, was what offended in the Gurney photo. Abraham Lincoln Presidential Library and Museum.

the inverse of our own. When Lincoln died in 1865, experience with
dead bodies was more commonplace than experience with photographic
images. The contemporary moment furnishes us with far more fluency
in the image and much less direct experience of the corpse. The photograph of Lincoln's body sits at the center of what was perhaps the first
"celebrity" death in America, and certainly the most widely mourned.
There is some relationship between its suppression and the emerging
mediated character of the mourning.

Lincoln also died in the midst of the transition from sovereign
power to mass democracy. Indeed, his time in office was characterized
by violent conflict over the inclusion of certain bodies in this mass—and
whether those bodies could legitimately be enslaved. His identification
with the body politic was therefore also shifting, from one in which
the body politic coincides with the body of the king to one in which
the body politic is distributed over the mass of democratic subjects.

The "political theology" of the king's two bodies names the difference between the leader's physical body, which ages and dies, and the
incorruptible and—crucially, for our purposes—*invisible* body politic.
During the age of absolute monarchy, these two bodies coexisted within
the body of the sovereign. His physical body was the visible body, but on
his death, this invisible and incorruptible body politic would be ritually
transferred to the body of a successor, hence the phrase "The king is
dead, long live the king."[19] In his classic study of the king's two bodies,
Kantorowicz makes it clear that this habit of thinking still permeates
political culture. We still think of the leader's physical body as both
congruent with yet conceptually separate from his office. The shock
of Lincoln's assassination was the violence it did to the body politic
as well as the physical body of the leader. What the mourning rituals
did was to ritually escort Lincoln's earthly body to the hereafter, while
preserving the integrity of the body politic.

In a democracy, however, the body politic is also distributed, as it
were, over the bodies of the citizens. Eric L. Santner creatively connects the various shifts identified by Foucault and Freud in the manner
of policing bodies with this change, citing the normative pressure of
this invisible body politic as the impetus behind the regulatory measures of biopolitics, on one hand, and their breakdown in neurosis, on
the other.[20] In other words, it is not merely the health and growth of

populations that give these disciplines their urgency but also the health and growth of the body politic, which is now no longer contained in the body of the sovereign but distributed throughout the population.

Santner writes that the "resources of representation"[21] available to subjects under such conditions will determine whether subjects are able to manage the normative pressure of assuming the body politic—the responsibility of social roles and governance of the self—or whether they will break down, like Freud's Dr. Schreber, who found himself unable to discharge his duties as a judge precisely because of his psychotic fantasies.[22] When it comes to death and the nation, therefore, it is worth asking what kinds of representational resources are called on to cope with the death of a leader. A photograph may be a useful resource, or it may feel inappropriate, depending on the historical and cultural moment. But in every case, the bodies of the populace will be strongly identified with the body of the deceased leader, not only because of the nation as corporation metaphor but because the body politic itself is at stake in the experience of national mourning.

With the advent of mass democracy, the political theology of the king's two bodies becomes secular, biopolitical. The Civil War marked an important shift in the body politic—enslaved bodies now become citizens, at least on paper. In its ambivalence toward the photographic image, Lincoln's death illustrates the difficulties inherent in that shift. To embalm and display Lincoln was, in some way, to attempt to make visible this invisible and incorruptible body politic—to body forth the eternal and unchanging nature of popular sovereign power. Embalming was at that moment a new "resource of representation"—a new way to figure the body politic, as it were. It perhaps felt appropriate to the moment in that a new body politic needed a new way to represent itself. Thus the photography, otherwise a completely normal "resource of representation" for mourning (at that time), becomes uncanny. It threatens with an independent ontology the ritual passage of the body from death to disappearance and memory.

Embalming Lincoln made the representational claim to depict the body politic, but it also disavowed that claim by folding the embalming into a funeral ritual that would eventually allow the body to disappear and the body politic to ritually return, as it were, to the mass democracy. Remember that the king's body politic is his *invisible* body—making the embalming and extensive viewing period an unusual exception wherein the physical body is equated with the body politic just long enough to ritually pass on.

The photograph of the body, conversely, is an explicit and permanent representation. The decision to suppress photographs of the body thus reads the photograph as having its own ontological existence, one that could threaten the relationship between the physical body of the president and the body politic of the nation. This understanding of the photograph depends on how its indexicality, or physical relationship to the referent, is read. For a better understanding of how photographic meaning depends on its reading, we need a brief detour through Peircean semiology. From there, we can continue on to our last two examples, which I argue are photographic renderings in the flesh, much different from Lincoln's embalming but with a similarly vexed relationship to the photographic image, whose potential polysemy threatens its privileged reference to a corpus.

PEIRCE'S INDEX AS A NATURALIZED REALITY PRINCIPLE

For Peirce, signification always implies reception. His theory of the sign classifies according to the nature of the relationship between the referent—the "real" thing in the world—and the sign. The index is defined by its causal relationship with the referent: the icon by likeness and the symbol by custom or habit.[23] Peirce explicitly classifies photographs as indexical because they are produced by a physical relationship between the light and the film. That is, photographs are witnesses rather than simply likenesses.[24] Crucially, Peirce's notion of "thirdness" requires that the index be *read* as such in order to function.[25] As Daniel Morgan carefully explicates, that audience requires certain conditions for the index to be read as such.[26] First, for a photograph to function indexically, it must indisputably refer to a reality "behind" it. We do not confuse the photograph with the thing itself but rather understand it to refer to something in the world. Second, the photograph must function as evidence of a *past* moment. This is again part of the referential quality of the photograph, that it attests to something that is necessarily past because it points beyond itself, but to something that is real (hence not an imagined future but a past reality). Barthes expresses this by saying that the photograph depicts "the *necessarily* real thing which has been placed before the lens." In contrast with the "chimerical" referents of discourse or literature, "in Photography I can never deny that *the thing has been there.*"[27] The emphasis here is not only on the reality of the image (the first condition) but on its pastness—"that-has-been."[28] Finally, a photograph can function indexically only if we understand how it was produced. We don't see photographs as evidence because they are faithful likenesses but because we know you can't photograph something that isn't there. This knowledge of the direct relationship between the image and the object is what gives us our certainty that what we see is a faithful likeness of what was in front of the lens.

André Bazin says that the photograph "embalms time," making a figure of form. This knowledge of the photograph's "process of becoming" is what gives it the "irrational power" to "bear away our faith."[29] Bazin's question is whether a photograph may be considered an object with its own ontology, separate from the object to which it refers. In a kind of performance of the credulity he ascribes to the photograph's audience, he cryptically asserts that the photograph *is* the model. As "time embalmed," the photograph creates another object, a monster neither purely referential nor independently "real." Whether or not this statement is metaphorical,[30] there is no question that photographs implicate and vex the relationship between the real and representation. This is why they are so important to consider in relationship with the corpse.

What the photograph does is liberate the object–model–referent from its temporal contingencies. Reading a photograph as an index, then, reveals an investment in the photograph as a secondary object, one whose existence is never independent but always tethered by means of physical causality to that which it represents. To put it more precisely, indexicality offers the logic of analogy the virtue of physical causation.

Embalmings also bear away our faith, and arguably more powerfully, because they appear to be nothing more than the very thing itself. Their indexicality is buried under the physical congruence of the referent and the representation (the body of the deceased). This is why Mrs. Lincoln could object so forcefully to photographs of her husband's corpse and not at all to that same corpse being viewed by thousands of strangers in person. Wittgenstein said that the "human body is the best picture of the human soul."[31] In the case of embalming, this statement is both precisely literal and scrupulously disavowed.

ENFORCING THE BODY OF LENIN AS PERMANENT REVOLUTION

Lincoln's embalmed body points to tensions between the embalmed body and the photographic image that will play out in different configurations in every corpus in this book. Whether and how the embalmed corpse is itself considered a visual object and thus a representational object will have different repercussions for its interaction with an increasingly complex and pervasive visual culture.

The next two examples develop this point by bringing the corpse as indexical sign to the fore. As we saw in the last chapter, corpses alone (without embalming or photography) are already representational objects with a complex relationship to the visual. They are the fleeting appearance of a departed presence; their visibility, both materially and culturally, is extremely limited. They are made to disappear, in the sense that their physical dissolution is both necessary for the social and (nearly) inevitable from a biological standpoint. When we have a corpse that does not disappear biologically—that is technologically manipulated so as to *appear* indefinitely as if it were recently deceased—then we have an object that is profoundly indexical. Its entire meaning stems from its physical relationship to an absent presence.

The corpses of leaders embalmed for public display represent the body of the nation in the medium of the flesh itself. Referent and sign coexist in the same physical space but not in the same time. You cannot, paradoxically enough, have a corpse without the (absent) presence of a living being. The corpse points toward the life that has just left it; it indicates absence. Embalming, to further tangle Bazin's words, photographs time—makes a picture of the corpse at the moment of its creation but rescues it quite literally from its "proper corruption."

At the same time, this referential bond weakens over time, as the physical body becomes more and more a technological creation and less and less a biological entity that relates to a departed soul. If Lincoln's body was able to refer to the deceased president over the course of the mourning period, it was because it was displayed in a culture that was still familiar with the visual signs of decay: a darkening of the skin, a sinking of the eyes in the sockets, and so on.[32] Visitors to Lenin's corpse, however, see a body that is as much wax, plastic, and cloth as it is flesh. There is an increasing danger that the corpse no longer refers to the grandeur of permanent revolution and instead offers the attraction of a wax museum or a freak show. This is because, for the corpse to remain visible—that is, recognizably congruent with the deceased person to whom it refers—it must be ever more rigorously maintained via technological and cosmetic manipulations. The process of chemical embalming may radically slow the effects of time, but decay cannot be completely halted. The preserved corpse must be maintained in particular ways if it is to remain visually recognizable. This point is easily grasped when one considers that a mummy of Lenin (his preserved flesh, but desiccated and darkened) would be an entirely different sort of attraction. As time goes on, the corpse embalmed for public display becomes increasingly an independent object whose reference is contested and polysemic.

Twenty-five years after the fall of Communist Russia, pilgrims and gawkers alike are drawn to Lenin's tomb in Moscow's Red Square. More than 10 million visitors have filed past the embalmed corpse, which has been on display since shortly after Lenin's death in 1924 (with brief interruptions during wartime). Guards enforce strict decorum: no loud talking, no laughing, no photographs or video; no hands in pockets, and all men must remove their hats. All the hush and reverence reserved for an audience with the dead is strictly observed, as if the great man had died only yesterday.

Why must this reverence be so strictly, even violently, enforced? It's because with every passing year, the corpse becomes more and more an object of morbid curiosity and less and less a stable referent to the historical Lenin. His embalmed corpse, preserved to make literal the ideal of permanent revolution within a particular national and historical context, now signifies in an entirely different context and to an entirely different audience.[33]

Lenin's corpse made visible the invisible body politic in a secular, modern revolutionary context that sought to redefine the boundaries of that body and its requisites for inclusion. It is no accident that most of the embalmed leaders are of either communist nations or in regimes with a strong cult of personality—or both. Lenin's image is all over even post-Soviet Russia; his corpse, however, makes a claim to the real that statues, posters, and lapel pins cannot. Even after the dissolution of the political body (the Soviet Union) of which this corporeal body is the literal emblem, that claim to the real is strong enough to thwart the periodic movements to bury Lenin underground. So long as the peripheral—we might say paratextual—elements can enforce that naturalized connection to the ideals that Lenin embodied, the corpse remains a viable symbol.

Eva Perón is the only woman embalmed for public display. She, too, was the central figure in a secular hagiography, and in a culture that sought to disentangle itself from its Catholic roots. Her body is the most fascinating body of the nation because it is gendered, doubled, lost, found, and hidden in plain sight.

"I BURIED HER STANDING BECAUSE SHE HAD BALLS!" THE CORPSE OF EVA PERÓN

Peronism reinvented social class in Argentina between 1945 and 1955 via the imposition of a complex iconography at once fascist and populist, authoritarian and revolutionary. Evita occupied center stage in what Jorge Luis Borges would later term a "crass mythology," a love story between the leader and his people mediated by the body of the beautiful, blonde actress whom he had chosen from among them.[34] Her corpse, therefore, embalmed for display in a monument to the Argentine worker, became Peronism's most powerful relic.

Now more than fifty years old, the embalmed corpse has "outlived" Evita the woman, who died at thirty-three. Originally intended for public display, the embalmed corpse was appropriated by the military when Perón was ousted in 1955, three years after her death. In the years that followed, the corpse was a key protagonist in the struggle between those seeking to eradicate the Peróns' long shadow in Argentine politics and culture and those seeking to return Perón to power. The military considered the corpse a state secret of the highest order and successfully hid it from the public for several years inside Argentina. According to the legend, the corpse carried a curse—which is perhaps why the military government eventually decided to take the corpse out of Argentina. They buried it in Italy, under the name Maria de Magistris.[35]

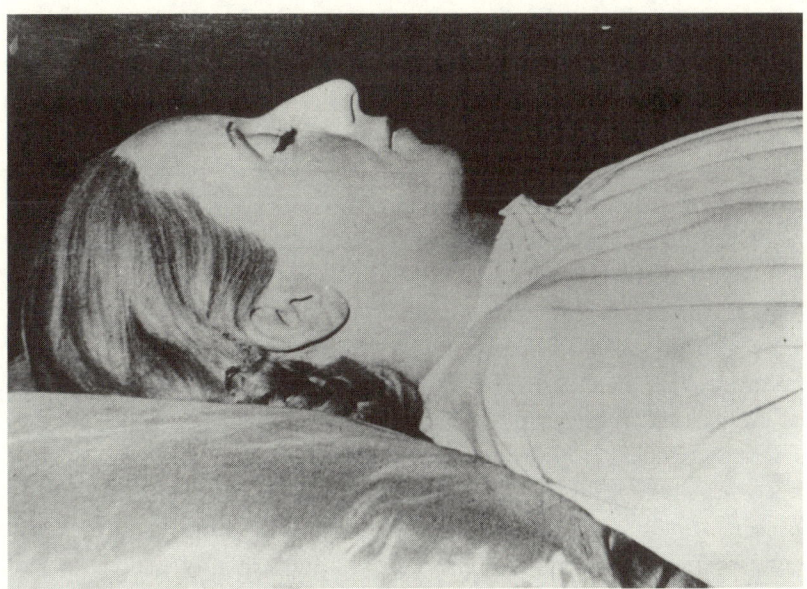

FIGURE 3. The embalmed corpse of Eva Perón, shown here before the body's theft and reburial. The embalmer, Dr. Pedro Ara, used photographs of Perón in life to "realistically" arrange her mouth over her protruding front teeth. Getty Images/Keystone.

Meanwhile, Peronist supporters on the left, including militant youth groups, equated the recovery of the corpse with the return of Perón himself. A period of escalating violence between the militants and the government culminated in the militants' kidnapping and execution of ex-president Pedro Aramburu. In the statement they sent to the newspapers, one of Aramburu's crimes was the theft and mutilation of the corpse of Evita. The government responded by exhuming the corpse and returning it to Juan Perón, who was at that time remarried and living in exile in Spain. This action only briefly satisfied the militants, who wanted the corpse returned to Argentina. They stole Aramburu's remains from the Recoleta cemetery in Buenos Aires and held them in ransom for Evita's. An aged Perón returned to power in 1973 and lived just long enough to disown the militant youth groups he had nurtured from exile and install his young wife as vice president, an honor that, twenty years before, Eva Perón had famously renounced under political pressure—a key moment in her hagiography.

So it was that in July 1974, Isabel Martínez de Perón, a forty-two-year-old former burlesque dancer, stood as president of Argentina on the balcony of the Casa Rosada, looking out at the crowds roiling beneath her. Perhaps she summoned the spirit of her predecessor as she tried to grasp what was happening. When Evita was exhumed, it is said that Isabel herself pulled out the crumbling hairpins, rusted after seventeen years underground, and with her own hands dressed the corpse's still-blonde hair.[36]

But the magic transfer never quite took. Isabel is remembered for only two presidential acts: first, the deployment of death squads to round up and execute the leftist groups that had brought Perón back to power, and second, the return and burial of the corpse of Eva Perón. Evita and Juan Perón lay in state side by side, his casket closed and decorated with military colors, hers glass lidded to show the perfectly preserved, white-clad corpse inside. She had Perón buried in the Chacarita cemetery, an appropriately proletariat place where victims of yellow fever had been buried in the colonial years. With a typically Argentine taste for historical irony (and an equally typical flair for revenge), Evita she buried eight feet deep in a mausoleum in the patrician Recoleta cemetery, the city of dead oligarchs, under the name of the father, Duarte, who had never recognized her as his own.

Shortly thereafter, Isabel was deposed by a military junta, and Argentina would suffer seven years of violent dictatorship. During this period of state terror, at least thirty thousand Argentines were kidnapped, tortured, and killed. With the return of democracy in 1983, Evita's legacy once more resurfaced and the long-suspended work of constructing her place in history began. The mausoleum that contains Evita's remains is one of the most popular sites of both tourism and pilgrimage in present-day Argentina. The mausoleum, marked with the Duarte family name despite that Eva's father never recognized her as his daughter, is a neoclassical anachronism in Buenos Aires's oldest and most wealthy cemetery. Its polished stone face is studded with plaques dedicated to Evita from labor unions and women's groups. A visitor on any day will find the iron grillwork covered in flowers, and on anniversaries in the Peronist calendar, the pile of offerings is so large that it blocks the narrow aisle between the mausoleums. But visitors cannot view the body, which is buried under the mausoleum and whose

FIGURE 4. The Duarte tomb in Buenos Aires's Recoleta cemetery, where Evita's corpse now lies. Associated Press/Sergio Goya.

vault, it is said, is guarded with two layers of double locked doors.

Lenin's corpse threatens to drift from its original anchor in the somberness of revolutionary hagiography because it has remained visible as time has passed and political circumstances have changed around it. Conversely, Evita's corpse cannot be seen except in photographs from the time of her death and her exhumation, when her corpse was displayed next to Juan Perón's casket at the time of his death. Most of the story of its "afterlife" takes place in secret—the allure was of a missing or disappeared corpse. Lenin's and Evita's corpses both endure beyond the "corpse time" conventionally allotted.

That endurance, however, need not be precisely on display for stable reference to a particular cultural memory to be troubled or—to use Deleuze and Guattari's language—for the corpse to deterritorialize the field of stable memory.[37] The fantastic chronicle of the corpse of Eva Perón threatens to overshadow the more "serious" memory of Eva Perón the political figure, humanitarian, and icon. Already the corpse itself undermines the indexical function of the photograph because it endures in time without photographic mediation. In this context, the documentary *The Unquiet Grave* seeks to reterritorialize the corpse's indexical function.

The Unquiet Grave

The 1997 television documentary *Evita: The Unquiet Grave*[38] figuratively "buries" the corpse by exposing the crimes committed against it and, by extension, against the memory of Eva Perón. The photographs of the corpse play a crucial role in this project and are thus the central node in the knot of reference and representation tethering Evita to her body. Bringing to light to put to rest is a common metaphoric operation in the aesthetics of public memory, and in Argentina in particular, it has resonances with the legacy of the period of state terror. Proof—and, crucially, *photographic* proof—of the corpse's desecration thus dispels the "disquietude" of its grave.

Directed by Tristán Bauer and written by Miguel Bonasso, two journalists with biographical and political ties to the militant Peronist left of the 1960s and 1970s, the documentary originally aired on Argentine public television on March 24, 1997. It scored an unprecedented twenty-six points in the ratings system and as a result was rebroadcast on March 29.[39] Since then, *The Unquiet Grave* has become a staple in yearly observances of Evita's death. It aired the night of July 26, when I was in Buenos Aires in 2002, which marked the fifty-year anniversary, and later that year, it screened as part of a retrospective titled "Eva Perón . . . esa mujer."[40]

Fifty years after Evita's death, the documentary *The Unquiet Grave* still works to tether the corpse to the leftist ideal of her legacy as a populist saint. Though it tells a story many know in its basic details, the film hinges on a big reveal of never-before-seen photographs of the corpse. These were taken by Juan Perón at the time of the body's exhumation in the late 1960s (when Evita had already been dead for seventeen years) and were obtained by Miguel Bonasso from an unnamed source. They document extensive damage to the corpse: a broken nose, a gash on the cheek, toes and feet split open and tarred. Rather than ascribe these "wounds" to the corpse's nearly two decades of peregrination, *The Unquiet Grave* uses indexicality to prove that these marks on the corpse were the result of mistreatment by the Argentine military.

Evita's sister Erminda wrote about the damage to the corpse in her book *Mi hermana Evita* (My sister Evita). However, these allegations were never corroborated, and Colonel Héctor Cabanillas, who supervised the burial and later exhumation of the embalmed corpse, insists that it was absolutely intact when it was exhumed. *The Unquiet Grave* features an on-screen interview with Cabanillas, the first time he has publicly spoken about the affair, where the aged military man reiterates that the corpse was perfectly intact and adds that his statement should put an end to any allegations to the contrary. From this interview, the documentary cuts to a reenactment of the act of photographing the corpse before moving into a sequence where the photographs themselves are revealed, showing Cabanillas to be a liar.

The re-creation of Perón taking the photographs cements this gesture toward the photograph as witness. We see a tight shot of (an actor portraying) Perón at waist level, his hands holding an old Roliflex camera, advancing the film with a hand crank, snapping the photographs. We don't see his face, only his hands and the line his belt makes at his waist between his pants and his shirt—the characteristically high pants and thick waist. The camera tracks from the dark hem of his jacket to

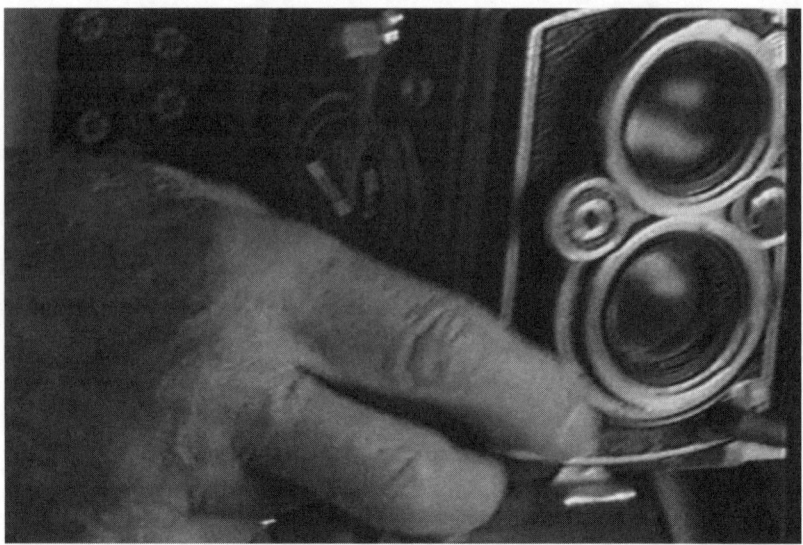

FIGURE 5. The act of photographing is re-created in Miguel Bonasso and Tristán Bauer's *The Unquiet Grave*. Screen capture.

his hand, turning the crank to advance the film. There's the sound effect of the "snap" of a photograph being taken, and the screen whites out as if with the light of the flash. We fade into a shot of the *lens* of the camera fading into an even tighter shot, with additional "snap" effects, settling finally on the flashbulb itself, which, as the final "snap" sounds, whites out the screen again. When the screen returns to color, we are seeing a curtain of reddish-blonde hair—now one of the actual photographs whose "process of becoming" has just been re-created.

Framing the photograph's introduction with this re-creation of the *act* of photographing clearly sets up an indexical reading wherein the lens is witness and the light is testimony. We see the camera; we hear a sound effect of a shutter snap; there is even a close-up of the lens to underscore its mechanical objectivity. The focus on the flashbulb and the whiteout effects all point toward an understanding of photography as "light writing"—and hence toward the traditional link between photography and truth.[41] *The Unquiet Grave* introduces its proverbial trump card by means of a framing mechanism that places the photographs of the corpse squarely within this tradition.

Recall that a photograph only has indexical power if the viewer is aware of how it is made, that is, if she knows to read it as an index.[42] Otherwise, it is merely iconic: a picture that resembles rather than a witness that testifies. *The Unquiet Grave,* working in an age when audiences have lost whatever naive trust they may have invested in the photograph, forcefully steers its viewers toward an indexical reading by re-creating the act of photography itself. The re-creation also points us back toward the past moment behind the photographs, the moment of inscription, here reanimated and thus all the more present and "real" for the viewer. Light itself is an actor in these re-creations, whiting out the screen entirely as though the audience itself were witness to the act of photographing.

Because the body is now buried and not on display, and because the mutilations were corrected before the body's last public viewing (in 1974; it was buried the next year and has not been exhumed since), these photographs provide special access to the precise moment of the corpse's existence when these mutilations were evident.[43] The narrative arc of the documentary, therefore, is a kind of exhumation and reburial—a translation[44]—whereby the burial "eight meters deep" no longer becomes a place of occultation of crime but a site of memory and pilgrimage to its "proper" referent, the woman Eva Perón.

The photograph and the corpse work together to create the implication that the mutilations are acts of violence committed against the body of the Argentine people. It is as if this body contains within it every tortured and disappeared body from the period of state terror. It does not, however, contain the many bodies tortured and disappeared under Peronism, or in its name. Hence a certain delineation of the nation and its honorable fallen is constructed in and around a photographic, that is, indexical, understanding of the corpse.

Index as Ideology

These contrasting examples illustrate the ways in which the causal tethering of indexical reference functions ideologically with regard to identity. As embalming's primary mode of signification, indexicality works to ensure that corpses like Evita's do not become unhinged from the identities and legacies of the people who once inhabited them. In the case of Evita, the long "afterlife" of the corpse and its many

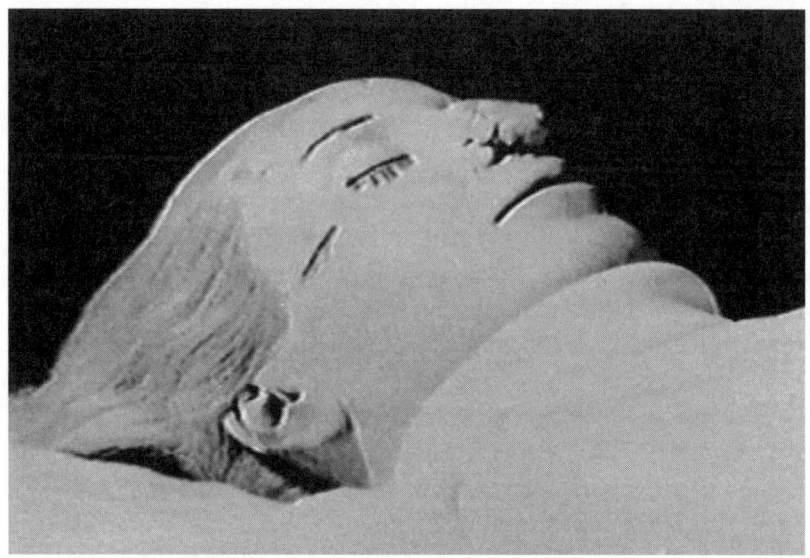

FIGURE 6. Photograph showing damage to Evita's corpse's nose and face. Screen capture from *The Unquiet Grave*.

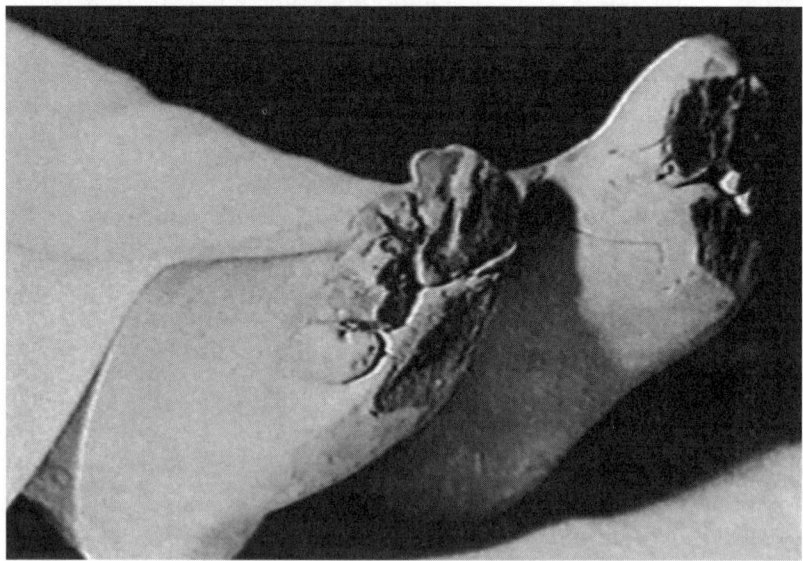

FIGURE 7. Photograph showing damage to Evita's corpse's feet. Screen capture from *The Unquiet Grave*.

adventures posed a threat to the stable reference because the corpse had its own narrative, which allowed it to signify beyond the specific context of Evita's life and legacy. Therefore, even as late as 1997, when *The Unquiet Grave* was made, there was a perceived need to return to indexicality as the mode in which to read the corpse. Nevertheless, this reading strategy had to be enforced, as we saw, by the explicit reference to the act of photographing and the flash, so that audiences already less convinced of the photograph's status as the "pencil of nature" would nevertheless revert to this dominant reading and take the outrages suffered by the corpse as equivalent to outrages suffered by Evita herself.

The political implications of such a strategy are clear: not only do identity and legacy become univocal within the documentary, but the polysemy of the corpse itself outside the frame of the narrative is foreclosed and disavowed. Here the political and material value of the legacy of Eva Perón as both a global icon of Argentina and a local political figure is at stake.

In both cases, however, the intent is to produce and maintain a stable relationship between the legacy of the deceased and the dead body. In this way, indexicality serves the ideological project outlined by Althusser: to interpellate subjectivity, even postmortem.[45] As the following chapters reveal, this interpellation comes up against complications in the fetishized corpses of figures whose bodies are either invisible or overly visible—and in those bodies whose metaphorical linkage to other investments and multiple affective vectors takes on the status of ontology.

THINKING THE CORPSE AS CORPUS

In *A Thousand Plateaus*, Deleuze and Guattari write of a kind of "nomad thought" exterior to the "arboresque," hierarchical thought of traditional Western philosophy. Arboresque or representational thinking delineates an enclosure by means of analogy: it pairs like with like, privileging common ground and excluding difference or what does not fit. Nomad thought, in contrast, works by affirmation and exteriority, meaning that it affirms and accounts for difference rather than carefully delineating a static identity. It communicates force, deploying vectors of contingent meaning rather than erecting solid hierarchies of truth.

This kind of thinking has consequences for the social in that we deploy representational thinking to understand ourselves and our place in the world. It is the dominant logos governing rigid boundaries between being, object, and concept. It regulates how we understand the self and also the selfhood of others both proximate and distant. Needless to say, it also structures our definition of the corpse as an object with a special relationship to the self. That's why it is easier to define the corpse by excluding the nonanalogous qualities, delineating an interior space of essence by expelling that which does not fit.[46]

To think the corpse nomadically would mean to define it by affirmation rather than negation, and to open thought onto the dynamic and differing contingencies in which it appears, not as an essence, but as a force, not as a hierarchically ordered unity, but as an assemblage. Nomadic thinking apprehends the corpse in its strangeness, accounting for its vectors of affect and effect in various fields or, as I have called them, corpuses—like the nation. Understanding the corpse in this way denaturalizes the representational couplings the embalmed corpse poses between identity, nationality, and alterity. It exposes them as representational rather than unproblematically truthful. It also renders the corpse's objecthood dynamic and situational rather than static and hierarchically fixed. If we take seriously Deleuze and Guattari's suggestion that arboresque or hierarchical thinking is reproduced at every level of the social, we can in this way begin to imagine death and the bodies it produces as a more mobile, contingent social reality, one in which the communicative force of difference is not subsumed under static hierarchies.

If thinking the corpse nomadically allows us to see it move and mean not as a concept or being or object (for it is clear that it slips easily from each of these traditional analytic categories), how might understanding the corpse as a dynamic and contingent process shift our attitudes toward death and remembrance? These are the social and political stakes of particular deployments of the corpse, deployments which, when thought differently, reveal both the work the corpse is asked to do in maintaining rigorous hierarchical modes of being and also the ways in which the corpse matters beyond these modes to create new, dynamic spaces of memory, identification, and loss.

The following chapters look at other, less explicit representational strategies for tethering the corpse to an assemblage of ideas, affects, objects, and images. Though the corpses in this chapter were embalmed bodies presented for public display, this is rather an exceptional use of the corpse. We next move to consider photographs of corpses, also an exceptional practice since the advent of modern embalming. These photographs are of two young boys: Emmett Till, who was lynched in Mississippi in 1955, and Hamza al-Khateeb, who was tortured and killed by the Syrian government in 2011. The graphic nature of the images combines with the indexicality of the photograph to produce a doubly indexical horror: both the image and the wounds on the body that it represents point toward an unseen terror and brutality. These martyred bodies mean as matter indexically, but the reality to which they refer is inherently unstable. Unlike the corpses displayed in an attempt to create a smooth and proper enclose of the nation, these corpses erupt in the public eye as a reminder of violent dismemberment of the nation. In turn, they are called on to do the work of nation building, of calling people together toward a common cause. As we will see, the encounter with the image is so volatile that it is difficult to assimilate into a narrative of social change. The martyred body is thus an encounter with death as annihilation and the image a relic of this sacrifice.

2

MARTYRED BODIES

Emmett Till and Hamza al-Khateeb

The relic makes meaningful matter out of martyred bodies. The word *martyr* comes from the Greek word for "witness": the martyr has witnessed something, a promise of a world to come or a reality of the world that is, and refuses to disavow it, even at the price of bodily suffering and death. Martyrs' remains are relics, carnal bits purified by suffering. Public, mass-mediated mourning is a ready-made reliquary, a televisual shrine wherein the visual remains become an iconography of the flesh.

The corpses considered in this chapter, Emmett Till and the Syrian boy Hamza al-Khateeb, are modern, secular martyrs; their relics are images. The nature of their deaths made them public figures; they were ordinary people, innocents, "sacrificial lambs"[1] whose deaths sparked civil uprisings.[2] Emmett Till, a black boy from Chicago who was lynched in Mississippi in 1955, became a martyr of the American civil rights movement when photographs of his mutilated corpse circulated in the black press. Half a century later, a YouTube video of the corpse of the Syrian boy Hamza al-Khateeb was used to make an appeal to the United Nations and Western humanitarian agencies to help the Syrian people in their struggle against a long-standing and brutal dictatorship. Both boys' corpses are sites of identification: they interpellate witnesses into a community, their solidarity becoming action in the name of a boy who could have been a son, a brother, a neighbor, a friend. Their images, though they circulate in very different economies of representation, are like relics in that they bear a physical (namely, indexial) relationship to a perceived martyr. The audience viewing the photograph comprises not just voyeurs but witnesses—persons with a direct relationship to the reality of what that body stands for. This relationship is one of responsibility: to act in solidarity with the martyred body by affirming the truth of his body as a witnessing text.

The mode of identification is to make the corpse excessively, disturbingly visible in death. This is the modality of the call—to make explicit the truth of the oppression that maimed these bodies and annihilated these young lives. These images circulated as image-relics of their sacrifice and as evidence of an appalling disregard for their humanity—and a call to action, in their name. Thus the hypervisibility of the corpses of these young innocents is crucial to their role as martyrs and points of identification for political and social action.

The reading of these explicit images is strongly indexical. The call to identify and respond depends for its power on reading the photograph as a faithful witness to a real event. The "realness" of that event is signified by the visible marks of suffering on the dead bodies of these young boys. These marks are themselves indices: they attest to a past act of violence by means of a physical relationship.

These hypervisual, strongly indexical images of corpses deviate from the traditional Western mourning practice in that nothing has been done to make the body appear to be at peace or to resemble the deceased in life. In this way, the bodies are images of death as suffering, not images of a particular person but of the wrongful violence: a photograph of evil. Rather than affirming life as it is, the corpse images of Till and al-Khateeb (and others like them) are used to make claims against dominant modes of social reproduction. They push past the boundaries of the control society, evoking death as its limit and its excess.[3] Rather than simply pointing to a past moment, these indexical images look forward toward social change and call on their viewers to inhabit different kinds of consciousness. They are revolutionary images where the materiality of the dead human body becomes the anchor in a counterhegemonic symbolic regime.

The use of the photographic image to "regard the pain of others" has a long history and has been debated by scholars as to its ethics and effectiveness (even Sontag argues with herself about this).[4] Here I ask what role the physicality of the body and its indexical signification in the photograph means at the heart of this matter. Sharon Sliwinski writes of a "virtual community" of spectators, whose "engagements with the pictures affected how human dignity came to be imaginatively extended to (and withdrawn from) distant others."[5] Drawing on Lyotard and others who explore Kant's assertion that the aesthetic judgment arises out of personal feelings and not from the universal faculty of reason, Sliwinski argues for an aesthetic of human rights wherein "justice [is] a principle that should not only *be* done, but also must be *seen* to be done."[6]

To claim that the images of these martyred bodies are *relics* identifies them as not only indexical but also ontologically separate from the deceased. Like the medieval saint's relic—a fragment of bone or skin, a sliver of the true cross—these photographic relics invoke the specter of the counterfeit precisely in their claim to authenticity. In this way, the images circulate in their own economy of meaning, one that ties them to discourses about suffering, alterity, identification, and community as well as ethical action. These images claim to make visible the suffering of an-other body so that this suffering may be imaginatively and affectively identified with a cause and a community. They invite us to imagine these boys' broken bodies as our own. At the same time, their graphic disfigurement distances us from their social identity, rendering them lumps of mutilated flesh. In their hyperreference to the corpse, then, these photographic relics make meaning out of their own matter. In so doing, they foreground the quandary of the body as a site of ethical action. Emmett Till and Hamza al-Khateeb both are and are not their bodies: we know very little of them, except for the graphic nature of their photographed corpses. As people, they belong to the memories of their families and to the imagination of those who identify with them. As bodies, they are not afforded the kind of privacy and decorum we normally extend to corpses *as remains*. That is, their bodies are asked to signify beyond the scope of their particular deaths via the creation of the photographic relic, thus rendering their personhood private and invisible.

In contrast to the highly visible but stylized corpses representing the bodies of the nation, these highly visible corpses stand for nations of dispossessed. They stand for peoples in a quest for sovereignty and recognition—and the overdetermined nature of their visibility, as relics, points to the ambivalence of that struggle. They are subversive images that cannot be easily domesticated or absorbed into larger narratives of becoming—hence, for example, the difficulty in properly situating Emmett Till's death in the history of the American civil rights movement. To acknowledge their existence without assimilating it to the logic of the same—to truly encounter the image as relic—means to face the violent fact of oppression, a fact that disrupts smooth narratives of liberation and social change.[7] These martyred bodies make torture and suffering real in their indexicality. In their representation of this reality, they are timeless; they erupt into the present moment and destroy any possibility of reparation or redemption.

It's important to think through the relationship these kinds of images forge between embodiment and representation because of this disruptive and annihilating power. If we need to "see" justice being done, in Sliwinski's formulation, how do these images work both for and against that social value? In what ways do these images disarticulate justice from material personhood, from the lived everyday experience of embodied humans?

EMMETT TILL AND THE AMERICAN CIVIL RIGHTS MOVEMENT

Fourteen-year-old Chicago native Emmett Till was lynched[8] in summer 1955 in Money, Mississippi, where he had gone to visit cousins. *Brown v. Board of Education,* the Supreme Court decision that legally ended segregation in education, had been handed down only the year before. The Montgomery, Alabama, bus boycott, often portrayed as the opening action of the civil rights movement, was yet a few months to come.

Till's mother, Mamie Bradley, had cautioned him about how he should treat whites in the South, where behavioral codes for black men were much different than in Chicago. Should there be any confrontation, even if he was in the right, he was not to "hesitate to humble" himself rather than risk a fight.[9] But, even so, she said she couldn't have conceived of what would happen to her son in Mississippi. Two white men kidnapped, tortured, and finally shot and killed him, weighing down his body and dumping it in the Tallahatchie River, after an incident in a store where he had some kind of interaction with a white woman that she interpreted as sexually aggressive. The body was so mutilated and damaged by three days in the water that Mose Wright,

Till's uncle, was only able to identify the body because he was wearing an initialed ring.[10]

The publicity surrounding Till's death and, most notably, the shocking photographs of his bloated and maimed corpse would bring lynching back out into the open. Indeed, as Hudson-Weems shows, lynching was a practice that was largely thought to have died out for those not living in the South.[11] In the South, the visibility and spectacle that had characterized lynching in the late nineteenth and early twentieth centuries had faded. When black bodies disappeared, and they often did, the rhetoric and narrative of lynching as spectacle served to perpetuate the power of lynching through absence and rumor rather than spectacle and publicity.[12] The nature of Till's "crime"—to disrespect a white woman—only fit the "punishment" if one adopted the standards of the Jim Crow South, where lynching was often justified as punishment for raping a white woman.[13] Moreover, the fact that Till was a child made the actions all the more shocking to northern blacks and whites alike. Although in the North, people lived with an everyday de facto segregation and racism, this violent enforcement of the South's much more rigid racial codes brought to light what many Americans in 1955 considered an ugly and barbaric anachronism.

Roy Bryant and R. J. Milem were charged with murder, which is remarkable enough in a society where such acts of violence routinely went unpunished, labeled as deaths "at the hands of persons unknown."[14] Another Jim Crow precedent was shattered when Mose Wright, Emmett Till's uncle, testified at the trial. Wright clearly identified the men as the same who had kidnapped his nephew, but no justice would ever come of it. The killers were acquitted in less than an hour by an all-male, all-white jury. Bryant and Milem would go on to sell their story to *Look* magazine for $4,000, unapologetically relating the horrific details of the slaying.[15] In this article, Milem claims that before he shot Till, he said, "Chicago boy, I'm tired of 'em sending your kind down here to stir up trouble. Goddamn you, I'm going to make an example of you."[16]

The Leflore County Sheriff's Department tried to bury the body immediately, but the Chicago family was alerted and applied legal pressure to have the body returned home. This was done only at Mamie Bradley's own expense, and with strict orders that they not open the sealed casket. As we will also see with Hamza al-Khateeb's corpse, the stakes of the decision to publish images of the corpse are made all the more complex by this official attempt to hide the circumstances of death and the condition of the corpse. Photographers from the black newspaper the *Chicago Defender* waited at the train station with Mrs. Bradley as she received the body of her son. The box was nailed shut and covered with seals from the State of Mississippi. Bradley insisted that it be pried open (a task of no small difficulty), there and then, so she could see her son's body and know that it was indeed he. That reporters were on hand to witness her reaction is the beginning of a story that sparked the civil rights movement.[17]

Bradley asked that when they prepared Emmett's body for burial, the funeral home not do anything to fix the corpse's gruesome appearance, so "all the world [could] see what they did to my son."[18] Even with this request, a few small things were done: the empty eye socket was stitched closed, and the tongue, which lolled hugely out of the corpse's mouth after the strangling of the fan wired around his neck, was removed and the mouth closed.[19] At the open-casket memorial in Chicago, an estimated one hundred thousand to even six hundred thousand saw the mutilated body. The casket was decorated with photographs of a smiling Till taken the Christmas before. These images made the horror of what was in the casket even more real. In the photograph, a grinning child dressed in his best suit leans against a television (at the time a luxury item) in a clearly middle-class home—supposedly, the security that first emancipation and then the Great Migration had won. In the casket was a maimed piece of flesh that seemed barely human. The message was clear: this joyful, blameless child was a lamb to the slaughter, and no black child was safe.

Photographs of the funeral, including a close-up of the corpse's face, were published in major black publications with both large local and national circulation: *Jet*, the *Chicago Defender*, the *Pittsburgh Courier*, the *New York Amsterdam News*, and the official NAACP publication, *Crisis*. This circulation among particularly northern blacks made Till's case a uniting incident in a still-nascent civil rights movement. For example, a *Cleveland Call and Post* poll found that five out of six major black radio preachers were preaching about Emmett Till and calling for change in the South.[20] NAACP membership and donations, which had been in decline since the antilynching movement of

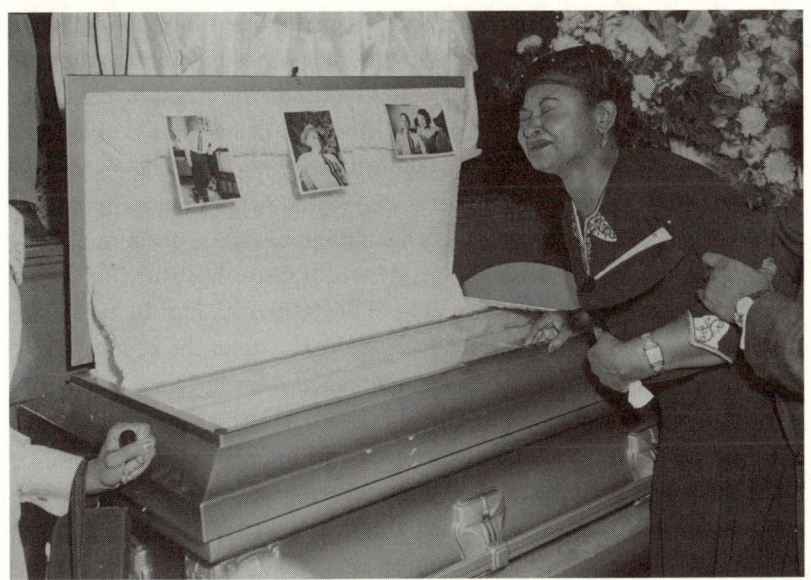

FIGURE 8. Mamie Till Bradley mourns her son. The photographs of Emmett Till in life pinned to the casket both contextualize him within a family and a community and also highlight his innocence and victimization. Associated Press/*Chicago Sun-Times*.

the 1920s, rose sharply as the NAACP played a central role organizing rallies and demonstrations all over the country, demanding justice for Emmett Till. The *Defender* sent a telegram to the president asking what he planned to do about the crime. Many who would go on to become major players in the civil rights movement wrote of the impact the images had on them—including Muhammed Ali, Joyce Ladner, and Chokwe Lumumba.[21]

Clenora Hudson-Weems argues compellingly that Emmett Till's death and the trial that followed it are overlooked as the seminal moment in the civil rights movement. The Montgomery bus boycott (which followed three months after Till's death), with its emphasis on nonviolent collective action, offered a more palatable spark, and Rosa Parks a less threatening heroine for that kind of movement. Nevertheless, Hudson-Weems shows that Till's lynching and the trial that followed deeply affected future leaders of the civil rights movement and sparked outrage and action among African Americans all over the country.

Central to organizing these actions, in addition to the NAACP, were labor unions, who mobilized working people in the North who thought that this kind of atrocity had been left behind on the plantation. Marnie Bradley herself articulated the way her son's death forged solidarity among African Americans: "Two months ago I had a nice apartment in Chicago. I had a good job. I had a son. When something happened to the Negroes in the South I said, 'That's their business, not mine.' Now I know how wrong I was. The murder of my son has shown me that what happens to any of us, anywhere in the world, had better be the business of us all."[22] Even those who did not attend the funeral could bear witness to Till's death via the published photographs. This act of witnessing forged a metaphorical link between the corpse and the wider community as well as a shared sense of meaning.

The image has long played a crucial role in making real the suffering of distant others.[23] Elaine Scarry has written of the supremely urgent moral imperative to communicate pain, an urgency only heightened by the impossibility of such a communication. Pain is a "world-destroying" force that defies language, which must rebuild the world if it is to inscribe and thus proscribe its infliction. The pain of torture, for example, is so utterly bounded and bonded within the body that it cannot be put into words and expelled. And yet no wrongdoing calls us more strongly toward the moral necessity of *telling*, of bearing witness. Experiences of violence and torture insist upon being told precisely to ensure that they occur "never again."[24] Against the world-destroying horror of torture, the witness remakes a world where that horror may be named and banished.[25]

The photographs of Emmett Till's corpse bear witness within this long tradition of ethical communication. As images, they can communicate differently than description, and as specifically photographic images, they do more than render: they attest.[26] Moreover, these images signified in the context of the complex relationship between lynching and photography. The images of Emmett Till's corpse are, for all these reasons, a "resource of representation" to make sense of this death. They take the matter of the corpse and make it mean in the larger context of the struggle for racial equality.

Fifty years later, the mediascape in which such an image could circulate is radically changed. The Internet and digital photography make possible instantaneous sharing to a global audience. It is in this context that the images of the dead body of the Syrian boy Hamza al-Khateeb circulate. The resources of representation are vastly different, but the aim is the same: to make real the suffering of a people via identification with gruesome images of the body of a martyred child.

Emmett Till's lynching challenges the ideological work needed to fold the legacy of the civil rights movement into the neoliberal, late capital narrative of a "post-race" society. There is nothing to be made of that image; it is a relic that holds us back from burying the corpse— and in a society obsessed with moving on from death and loss, this is unacceptable. The bald challenge that the protests of the civil rights era posed to white supremacy also stood in defiance against the economic colonialism that underwrote it. This contradiction must be resolved as the movement becomes part of "our" history. The social conditions under which Emmett Till was lynched have changed in certain ways, but economic and social racism persists. As long as we are taught that civil rights were an issue in the past that was resolved without violence (by figures such as King and Parks), the continuing violence, particularly against black male bodies, cannot be politicized. Hudson-Weems's writing is precisely intended to restore Till to that history, and the radicalizing shock of the encounter—which again I use in Deleuze's sense of an unassimilatable eruption of alterity[27]—with the image is crucial to understanding the effect.

HAMZA AL-KHATEEB AND THE SYRIAN CONFLICT

In late April 2011, a thirteen-year-old Syrian boy named Hamza al-Khateeb disappeared after joining in a nonviolent protest against the police siege of the town of Dera'a. His family's inquiries returned no confirmation of death or arrest. A month after the disappearance, the family received notice that their son was dead. He had been accidentally shot, they said, during the protest and had only now been identified. The body would only be returned on the condition of their silence: they must not speak to anyone outside of Syria about the circumstances of his death or the condition of his body.[28]

The reason for this stipulation was immediately obvious when they saw the body. There were cigarette burns on the arms and chest, the jaw and kneecaps were smashed, and the neck was broken. There were three bullet wounds, none of which alone would have killed him, meaning that his death was slow and painful and that he likely suffered torture beforehand. The final and most gruesome mutilation was that the boy had been castrated, either during the torture or postmortem.[29] This was clearly not an accidental shooting. This child had been brutally tortured—systematically and repeatedly—during his monthlong disappearance.

In returning the body and stipulating the gag order, the Syrian government clearly meant to terrorize the family. Amazingly, this act of inhumanity had the opposite effect. The family mobilized their outrage and grief to contact an activist, who made a video of the body. In addition to this visual evidence, an off-camera voice detailed and explained the marks of torture and mutilation. The voice-over also makes explicit what the marks only indicate: that this was an act of deliberate and appalling horror.

Al-Khateeb's family consented to have the video posted on YouTube in May 2011, as part of an effort to publicize the atrocities committed by the Assad administration. This brave action had impact both locally and internationally. In the town of Dera'a, where al-Khateeb had disappeared, protests erupted only hours after the video appeared online.[30] As protests continued in Syria, people began carrying signs with al-Khateeb's photograph on them and using the slogan "We Are All Hamza al-Khateeb." At the time of al-Khateeb's death, the protests in Syria had been going on for only about six weeks, and the video seemed to give new life to the movement.

The autopsy video of Hamza al-Khateeb was first uploaded to YouTube in May 2011. As a document, the video's main strength is not its iconicity, because the resolution is extremely poor: the footage was taken using a mobile phone.[31] The handheld, pixelated image shows the boy's naked, mutilated body lying on a plastic sheet and scattered with flower petals. The videographer circles the body, occasionally zeroing in on details such as bullet holes. At times, a plastic-gloved hand can be seen gently lifting an arm or turning the head to better indicate evidence of wounds and torture. Throughout the video, an off-camera voice narrates the images, effectively subtitling them as evidence of torture and demanding, "Where are the human rights committees? Where is

FIGURE 9. A woman protests outside the Syrian Consulate in Sao Paulo, Brazil, with a photograph of Hamza al-Khateeb in life juxtaposed with an image from his autopsy video. Agencia Estado via Associated Press/Daniela Souza.

the International Criminal Court?"[32] Though the video was initially taken down because of its graphic content, a slightly edited version is still available, which blurs images of the severed genitals and carries a warning about explicit content.[33]

Protests erupted in the cities of Dera'a, of Ma'arat an-Numan, and of Hama within four hours of the video's first appearance online,[34] and a reported sixty-three people were killed that day, making it the bloodiest protest yet at the time.[35] Although the government responded almost immediately by shutting down Internet service, the video was also aired by Al Jazeera, which expanded its reach beyond those with computer literacy and access.[36] On Friday, June 3, 2011, protestors carried signs with al-Khateeb's picture during a march that organizers called "Children's Friday."[37] Shortly after the video went viral, a Facebook page titled "We Are ALL Hamza al-Khateeb" was created by activists both in Arabic and in English. Within the first week of its creation, the page had sixty thousand followers.[38]

English-language news sources also picked up on the video, referring to al-Khateeb as the "face" of the Syrian revolution.[39] In the United

States, the *Huffington Post* did a small segment on the video,[40] and a longer story ran in the *New York Times*.[41] Anderson Cooper devoted the "Keeping Them Honest" segment of his CNN newsmagazine *Anderson Cooper 360* to the Syrian conflict on May 31, airing video of both the corpse and the protests in al-Khateeb's name. The "Keeping Them Honest" segment also included secretary of state Hillary Clinton's remarks about the incident, which she said "symbolizes for many Syrians . . . the total collapse of any effort by the Syrian government's [*sic*] to work with and listen to their own people."[42] Clinton's remarks also echoed the sentiment expressed in most English-language stories about al-Khateeb and the video of his corpse: that this death was symbolic for Syria, and that the circulation of the video would inevitably lead to stronger and stronger evidence of atrocity, greater moral authority for the peaceful protestors, and the eventual resignation of President Assad. In the years that have passed since the video first appeared, however, this has manifestly not been the case, nor have there been follow-up news stories about al-Khateeb or his family, who were detained after they defied the government by making the video.

As of this writing, Syria continues to unravel, with *massacre* becoming a word used in Western press coverage, along with *civil war* and *atrocity*. This makes the actual political situation a moving target, particularly as evolving situations in Egypt, Lebanon, and Turkey are beginning to call into question the Western perception of the so-called Arab Spring as an instance of successful peaceful popular uprising. The focus here is thus restricted to this particular video and the ways in which it has been used to make a metaphorical connection between one corpse and the plight of an entire nation. As will become clearer as I analyze the video in more detail, the audience is outside Syria and Western: the voice of the activist calls on the United Nations, and the original posting was subtitled in English.

The corpse here serves to indexically document violence and injustice, surely, but it also moves beyond the status of "deceased subject" to become a symbol for violence and oppression themselves. Whether distributed via Facebook or YouTube or by more traditional outlets such as Al Jazeera, the images of the corpse forge a figurative link between this corpse as a human sustained in a network of other lives who was violently made into this unthinkable *thing in the world,* this material testament not only to the boy himself and to his family's bravery but also to the reality of violence, death, torture, and mutilation. The corpse itself is what makes the unthinkable legible and brings it into view, however strategically or briefly.

IMAGE CIRCULATION: PUBLISHED PHOTOS AND YOUTUBE VIDEO

The images of Till's corpse published in *Jet* magazine (September 15, 1955) appeared fully captioned by the larger story of Till's lynching and with photographs of him together with his family. In this context, the identity of Emmett Till as a person with a family and whose death was singularly tragic is foregrounded. Mamie Bradley's decision to keep the casket open and to publish the photographs is also part of the story as presented in *Jet*. It is impossible to separate the images of the horribly mutilated body from a mother's grief.

This context allowed readers to bear witness to the suffering of one black body as the suffering of any and all black bodies. This is particularly important because lynching acts out a sadistic fantasy of control of bodies, of punishing bodies that transgress. The *Jet* photographs preserved Till's social identity, his particularity as a son, as a teenager, as a Chicagoan, and so on. He was not an anonymous victim, and the photographs respected his personhood. Yet they also convoked an identification where part of the horror of the crime was its random nature, that Till could have been anyone. The contrast between the photographs of Till in life and the images of the corpse serves to make this paradox—a particular someone who is nevertheless anyone—part of the outrage. As Elizabeth Alexander writes, "Till's body was ruined but nonetheless a body, with outlines that mean it [could] be imagined as kin to, but nonetheless distinct from, our own."[43]

Most importantly, however, the layout and captioning of the *Jet* images framed their meaning as strongly indexical, much like the re-creation of the act of photographing in *The Unquiet Grave*. The headline reads, NATION HORRIFIED BY MURDER OF KIDNAPPED CHICAGO YOUTH. There is a four-page spread; before we get to the shocking image, there are photographs of Till in life and of his family members, thus situating him as part of a family now struck by grief. At the bottom of the third page is a two-part image. On the left is a photograph of Bradley and a man who is not identified in the caption. In the foreground of the image is the casket, with the mutilated face just visible above its edge. The man is holding Mrs. Bradley by the shoulders and around the waist and staring directly into the camera with a fixed and enraged expression. Bradley gazes down and to the right at her son's face. Her body is slack; it looks as though her companion may be supporting her. Immediately to the right of this image is a close-up of the mutilated face. The caption reads, "Mrs. Bradley got first look at brutally battered son in undertaker's morgue. More than 600,000, in an unending procession, later viewed body." The framing here takes us to the moment of disclosure from the *point of view of the mother*—that is, our "first look" at the corpse is also hers. The juxtaposition of the images has a cinematic look to it, as if to show us, in the right-hand image, precisely what we see her seeing in the left one.

This sequence thus reinforces the photograph's indexical power to point to a specific moment in the past. The shock and horror of the image and its relevance to anyone who bears witness are underlined by this depicting of the moment of seeing, or of the mother's gaze, which we are invited to inhabit. This prepares us for the next page, where the corpse itself is shown as "mute evidence."

The next page is entirely dominated by a terrifying close-up of the mutilated face. "Close-up of lynch victim bares [*sic*] mute evidence of horrible slaying. Chicago undertaker A. A. Raynor [*sic*] said youth had not been castrated as was rumored. Mutilated face of victim was left unretouched by mortician at mother's request. She said she wanted 'all the world' to witness the atrocity."[44]

Years after the death, Bradley would define the notion of an eruption or an encounter that cannot be assimilated to previous ideas of the world. She writes, "People had to face my son and realize just how twisted, how distorted, how terrifying race violence could be. People had to consider all of that as they viewed Emmett's body. The whole nation had to bear witness to this."[45]

This bearing witness had to happen through the image and not through description. The image itself was a way of making real something that is beyond comprehension in its brutality. Mamie Bradley again: "I knew that I could talk for the rest of my life about what happened to my baby, I could explain it in great detail, I could describe what I saw laid out there on that slab at A.A. Rayner's [the funeral home], one piece, one inch, one body part at a time. I could do all of that and still people would not get the full impact. . . . They had to see what I had seen."[46]

Supporting this assertion, Harold and DeLuca claim that "the *image* of Emmett Till's monstrous and grisly body could not be ignored. It served as graphic testimony to the brutal race hatred in the 1950s South in a way that written text never could have done. It allowed viewers to become witnesses to what for many had existed only as rumor and legend."[47]

The community of readers formed by the circulation of *Jet* magazine and other black publications thus encountered the body in a way that did not allow it to be assimilated to other forms of knowledge. This body erupted in the eyes and imaginations of its readers as "viscerally, terrifyingly real." This framing of the image moved it outside of representational thinking—that this body is like another body, or this killing is like any other—into a nomad thought, an encounter that cuts across existing regimes of representational thought and confronts the viewer with its brute honesty.

This nomad image, which cuts across any gridded space of intelligibility, has its own powers to create a world, to create "a temporary nexus around which people could link themselves to each other in a new network, thus reconfiguring their agency in powerful ways."[48] Rather than rejecting the corpse as abject, the community identified with the abjection and "embraced Emmett in all his abjection and made his body *mean* differently"[49]—that is, it does not signify as a warning or as fearful but "illustrated that their very *bodies* were at stake."

These were the representative resources used to make sense of the death of Emmett Till. The photographs of the corpse were used precisely to cast the murder as a lynching and thus situate it strongly within the framework of racial violence and inequality. And they were used indexically—that is, their depictions depended for their impact on their being read as pointing to a reality that *had been*. The corpse itself, in other words, is allowed to be a fleeting entity here. The strength of the photograph is that it captures a moment before decomposition and after death, a moment that would (and should) otherwise quickly fade into the anonymity of dissolution and decay. This is why, in Kristeva's classic formulation, corpses are abject: they are liminal objects that must maintain the illusion of wholeness by being ritually ushered into disappearance, held at a distance, for fear of contamination.[50] By photographing and witnessing the mutilated corpse, the black community captured and witnessed this abjection. They understood it as constitutive of their community, as a political undertaking to seek recognition, and, at the same time, in acknowledging and embracing the abject corpse, they were able to find a place within their community to symbolically situate Till's loss and thus continue on in his name.

HAMZA AL-KHATEEB: EMBRACING THE ABJECT FOR A GLOBAL AUDIENCE

The YouTube video is titled *Martyr Hamza alKatib The Child 13 Years Old,* and the image carries a logo of the Syrian Free Press, which is a nonprofit news organization created in 2011 by human rights activists. There is no reference to Syria in the title, so one would have to click on the video to see the Syrian Free Press logo. The name of the video also appears in Arabic script, so this would perhaps be a signal that the video came from the Middle East. No family members appear in the video, nor is the narrating voice identified. The video from the start focuses on the fact that this boy is a child martyr but provides little else to ground the corpse as a deceased subject. We know his age and his hometown, and his activities in the hours before his arrest, but nothing more of his life or family. This treatment of the corpse as thing—as an index for the violence of the Assad regime, a metaphor for the suffering of a people, and a plea for humanitarian action—stands in sharp comparison to *Jet* magazine's treatment of Till, which situated the boy in a family and whose circulation ensured a particular audience with some shared characteristics. Al-Khateeb's corpse is there as an index of cruelty; his martyrdom is not presented as its own reward, but his loss as a person takes a backseat to the evidence that his body presents of the human rights abuses of the Assad regime.

Though the male off-camera voice is sometimes clinical, and in some versions the video is labeled an autopsy (though the body is never cut open), his narration of the condition of the corpse is polemical at a variety of levels. First of all, the voice-over begins with an invocation

FIGURE 10. Abriel Thomas, a cousin of Emmett Till, displays childhood photos of Till in 2004, after the Justice Department reopened the murder investigation into his death. Contemporary circulations of Till's image are usually of the corpse only and rarely situate him within family and community, as this one so poignantly does. Associated Press/Jeff Roberson.

of God's name, thus positioning the civil disobedience of the activists (who act in defiance of the Syrian government's gag order) as subject to a higher law. The narration further indicts the government actions in its clear identification of wounds and marks of torture—injuries that would have caused great suffering but likely not immediate death. By reading the marks of the corpse as deliberate acts of torture, the video and its narration again foreground the indexicality of the image by guiding the viewer to an indexical reading of the wounds: this burn points to torture with a lit cigarette, these bruises indicate that his kneecaps were smashed, and so forth. The narration thus strongly guides the viewer to a response via a clinical, descriptive style that mimics the unquestionable "truth" of indexicality.

As the video progresses, the narration moves from simple documentation of wounds to a more "editorial" tone, especially when referring to the most shocking mutilation, the body's castration, which he calls "grotesque." From here the narration moves to open condemnation of the Assad regime, calling Assad a traitor, followed by an indictment of the international community in its failure to respond to a humanitarian crisis. The video closes with a statement of the date, again returning to the mode of pure documentation, of letting the images speak for themselves as proof of atrocity:

> In the name of God, the Compassionate, the Merciful: We bring you another martyr to freedom. He came from the city of Al-Jizah, in the province of Dera'a. His name was Hamza 'Ali al-Khateeb. He was 13 years old. He came out on a Friday of Anger [dedicated to] raising the siege on the people of Dera'a. He was arrested in the area of Sayda. He was then tortured in the most heinous fashion. Look at the marks of torture. This was a bullet, shot through his right arm. It exited the arm here. It exited from here, and entered his torso here. Here [you see] a round in his abdomen. Another round in his left arm, parallel to his right. Once again, the bullet exited his arm and entered his torso. Then, there's another bullet that entered his upper chest. Now look at the bruising along his face. If this were not enough, his neck has been broken. Now, look at the bruising on his right leg. In addition, there is [something] more grotesque. This degree of torture wasn't enough for them. They castrated him, too. Then they sent a round of bullets through him. [Image blurred] His penis has been cut off. They cut it off. Look at the reforms Bashar the traitor has called for. Where is the [UN] Human Rights Committee? Where is the International Criminal Court? Where are all those advocates of freedom? "There is no help, no strength but in God" [proverb quoted in times of distress]. The date is May 25, 2011.[51]

I want to be clear that when I describe the ways in which the narration frames and captions the images, what I am describing is not a direct, aural experience of listening to the off-camera voice. Rather, what I am describing is what a non-Arabic speaking YouTube listener would experience: a visual, linear reading of English subtitles which appear at particular intervals below the images on the screen and which relate to the aural experience of listening to the off-camera voice, but in nonspecific ways. That is, it's clear that the subtitles are representing the words spoken by the off-camera voice and that when he finishes speaking a phrase, what appears on the screen is a translation of those words. Nevertheless, it is beyond the possibility of an average English-speaking viewer to evaluate the correspondence of even a particular phrase to its

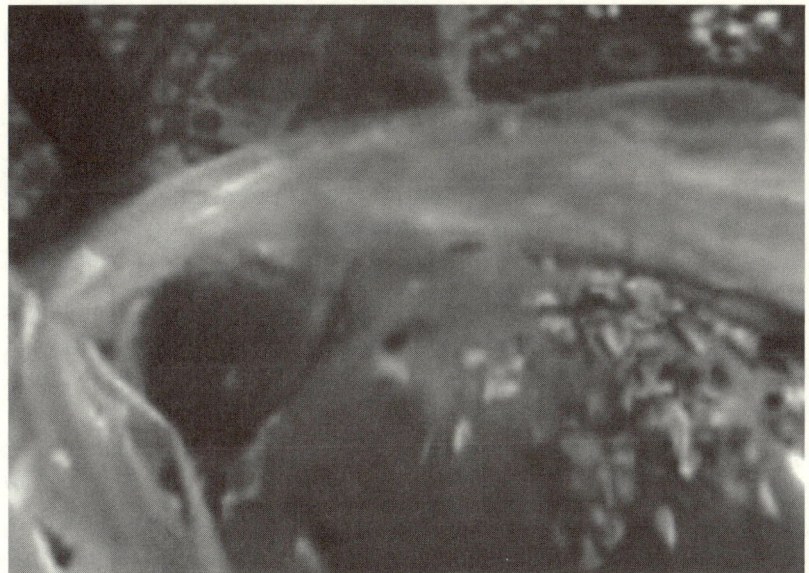

FIGURE 11. The body of thirteen-year-old Hamza al-Khateeb, scattered with flower petals, in the autopsy video circulated on YouTube in 2011. Associated Press/APTN.

translation, let alone whether the translation is accurate, if such a thing even exists. In this sense, I think it's important to consider that whoever authored the subtitles did so with a Western audience in mind. As I will discuss in more detail, certain remarks are added parenthetically to the subtitles to either clarify syntax or, in one case, identify cultural meaning. As I analyze the video, then, I explicitly engage it as a text in translation made for an audience who is linguistically and culturally other than the language and culture of its production.

The video opens on a close-up of al-Khateeb's face. This image is also the screen capture that is most often reproduced in news stories about the boy's death and its symbolism. Al-Khateeb's eyes are closed, and his face is slack. His cheeks are smooth and childishly round, even pudgy. The resolution quality is so poor that it isn't immediately clear how to read the round cheeks, and their color, which is brownish deepening to purple. Not knowing how he looked in life, the swelling in the cheeks and the skin color do not immediately signify swelling and bruising, though as the video unfolds, it becomes clear that this is the case.

The video thus begins with the personhood of al-Khateeb, that is, with his face, but that face is already marked with violence. Unlike in the *Jet* pictorial, there is no picture of al-Khateeb in life, nothing to compare with this broken body, which the voice-over is directing us to read as an index not of suffering (though there is that) but of wrongdoing.

As it widens from close-up into medium, the opening shot establishes that the body lies, naked, on a plastic sheet scattered with flower petals. It is unlikely that he was embalmed, but as has already been argued, the preparation and care of the corpse is a cultural practice that mediates the body, making it a representation of the person who just died and not, for example, of the agony of death itself, or the fear. This is another way in which the video frames al-Khateeb as a person and not just as a lump of mutilated flesh. Paradoxically, it is the fact that he's been treated as such—as an object on which violent power may be exercised arbitrarily—that occasions this postmortem assertion of his dignity. Honoring the body thus both highlights its fragility and uplifts its piteous mortification.

Over the opening image, the off-camera voice begins, "In the name of God, the Compassionate, the Merciful." This phrase is a common translation of the Islamic phrase known as the Bismillah. The Bismillah is an invocation of God's name, a verse repeated several times in the Koran. The Bismillah appears in daily prayers and is also inscribed on gravestones and on monuments dedicated in the name of a deceased person. It is a common element in everyday Islamic life, where it is required before eating, for example, but it may be recited as an invocation of the divine at the start of any action. Significantly, the Bismillah is usually the opening phrase of the constitution of Islamic nations, including Syria's. Here the cameraman's recitation of the Bismillah firmly situates his actions within a law and ethics removed from that which held al-Khateeb's family to the gag order. Its use here mocks the Syrian regime's claims to divine legitimacy and Islamic ethical standards.

Having invoked God's blessing for his undertaking, the cameraman identifies the body as "another martyr to freedom." Here again, the rhetorical framing of the video presents the law that was violated (the gag order) as invalid against the divine purpose of the protestors, who are martyrs. He then identifies the body by name—Hamza Ali al-Khateeb—and states his age, thirteen, and where he came from. As these details are narrated, the camera pulls back to reveal a dark spot on the body's bare chest: clearly a bullet hole. As the name Hamza Ali al-Khateeb is spoken, the camera focuses in an increasingly tight close-up on this wound. It then moves back to a middle distance above the body and zooms in to another bullet wound, this one on the arm, as the voice-over briefly narrates the events leading up to al-Khateeb's death: he went to a peaceful demonstration, he was arrested in a specific place.

Then, the voice-over says, "he was tortured in the most heinous fashion." This comment and the opening identification of al-Khateeb as a "martyr to freedom" (before he is even named) serve to frame the somewhat forensic nature of what follows. By identifying al-Khateeb as a martyr before even giving any other details of his life and death, the filmmaker is asking audiences to read his death as sacrifice for a greater cause. The almost clinical task of documenting the marks of "heinous torture," then, is also cast as an act in the service of the greater good rather than as a gory spectacle or desecration. In life al-Khateeb is a martyr; in death his body is also enlisted to the cause, offered to the camera's scrutiny as sacrifice.

The next sequence is devoted to precisely this: to showing the wounds on the body. The voice-over begins by simply saying, "Look at the marks of torture." This demonstrative gesture signals a shift from the linguistic to the visual register. The narration up until this point worked to contextualize the image—to give a name to the body, to tell the story of how he came to die. Now the narration asks us simply to bear witness.

This is not an easy task. The marks on the body register terrible violence, even with the poor resolution of the cell phone camera, even with the postproduction blurring of the image of al-Khateeb's castration. What we are asked to witness is unspeakable, staggering.[52] This is the appeal made by the imperative to witness which the video of Hamza al-Khateeb so precisely articulates. See this thing that is impossible to see, from which any sensible human would turn away. See it, and in so doing, bear witness with your horror to the evil it represents.

This sequence documents the bullet holes in both arms and both sides of the torso, the broken neck, and the smashed kneecaps. The camera is very close in to each of these wounds, and often there is a hand in the shot, with a finger pointing to what we need to see. This is the rhetoric of witnessing at its most assertive: the verbal imperative to see underlined by close camerawork and, as if that were not enough, by pointing. One is struck by the gentle way the hands move to touch the body, move the arms or head to point something out. We don't know whose hands they are; we don't know if they are the hands of the man operating the mobile phone, or of the man who is speaking, or if all of these, hands, camera, and voice, are one person. But we are struck by the interface between the living and the dead, between the gentle care taken in showing these wounds and the horrible, human-inflicted violence they register.

In the final sequence, language reemerges to frame what is perhaps the ultimate horror: the sight of al-Khateeb's castration. Here is where the off-camera voice calls Assad a "traitor," where he calls upon the United Nations Human Rights Committee and the International Criminal Court. This sequence is thus clearly addressed to distant others, to those who may listen and watch and have some ability to affect decisions made in these international bodies. This appeal to international law and to the concept of human rights is juxtaposed with images that are simultaneously graphic and unclear. The camera focuses very tightly on the castrated genitals and holds there for the duration of the remarks. It is no longer possible to see the original video, without censorship. However, even with the postproduction blurring effect,[53] it is possible to realize that one is looking at testicles and that there is a large, black wound where the penis should be. The image fills the frame. There is no place to look away, while the voice calls on the legal and juridical "advocates of freedom" who have abandoned this child to his piteous fate.

This sequence ends with the quotation, "There is no help, no strength but in God," which is followed by the parenthetical explanation "proverb quoted in times of distress." This proverb comes from the Koran and is often used when someone dies. The ending quotation thus forms a bookend with the opening Bismillah, situating the actions of the videographer firmly within divine authority rather than in the law of the land. However, while the Bismillah is not explained with any parenthetical comment, the bracketed explanation of the proverb is clearly intended for a Western, non-Muslim audience to better understand the emotional register of the moment.

It's not until after this phrase has been uttered that the camera moves back and the genitals are carefully covered again with a white cloth. The voice states the date, and the video ends.

"We Are ALL Hamza al-Khateeb"

Because the video was on YouTube, the response was not merely local but international. In response to the video, Clinton's statement arguably sidestepped the matter, because it addressed to the video's symbolic impact and not so much its allegations of torture and murder. In speaking to the video's symbolic power, Clinton underscored its affective work. She spoke to the way the video mattered to Syrians: that it symbolized for them their government's utter failure, its illegitimacy as a democratic or constitutional political entity. Clinton's framing of the issue echoed ongoing conversations about the use of social media and the Internet in the so-called Arab Spring. Internationally, the story was about the way that viral videos and Facebook and Twitter accounts were mobilizing local unrest, grief, and outrage.

One result of the video's impact was the creation of the Facebook page titled "We Are ALL Hamza al-Khateeb." Fifty-eight thousand to sixty thousand people visited the page in the first days after al-Khateeb's death; the English version garnered three thousand friends in its first few days in operation.[54] There are now twenty-five thousand friends of the page, according to a posting on June 26, 2012.

As the page's name suggests, identification on the part of the distant or perhaps particularly on the part of the Western Facebook user is framed as a gesture of solidarity with the people of Syria. It is because of the images of his corpse and their wide circulation that al-Khateeb became that point of identification for the site. Nevertheless, the site itself has moved on from showing the video, to which it does not link. Indeed, the corpse of Hamza al-Khateeb is not necessarily the image most associated with the Syrian resistance. That is, although the video itself did initially circulate widely and generate an impassioned response, it's also the case that this graphic image has receded with time from the public campaign using his death as a point of identification.

The profile picture of the Facebook page (in both Arabic and English) is not the corpse but what looks like a school photograph, a headshot, of al-Khateeb in life. In a process that mirrors Barbie Zelizer's analysis of the video of Neda Agha-Soltan's death in Egypt, the "face" of "We Are ALL Hamza al-Khateeb" is not the face of the corpse but a picture taken in life.[55] Crowds of protestors have been seen carrying this image in Syria as a reminder of all that al-Khateeb's death symbolizes— in short, as a way to make literal this process of identification. Here the photograph functions in what Zelizer has identified as "the subjunctive voice of the visual."[56] The information section of the Facebook page clearly identifies al-Khateeb as a boy killed by the Syrian regime. His photograph is thus captioned with death: his somewhat awkward smile and too-neat hair, which under ordinary circumstances would have been the banal hallmarks of a school picture, are now wrenching details of a life about to be cut short. Al-Khateeb the posthumous revolutionary, then, is not a corpse but an image of someone "about to die."

A typical posting is likely to include graphic footage, often of children.[57] It usually includes a plea to publicize the post—to "Like" it, to repost it. Posts often also address the United Nations and the international community, asking for intervention and aid. As the conflict has continued, these pleas also comment on current measures, critiquing them as being inadequate or even counterproductive. A video from June 1, 2012, shows the body of a man burned alive. The voice-over says, "Thanks very much, Mr. Annan, for your grace periods," and the English subtitle also includes the comment "sarcasm" in parentheses, for those of us who cannot read the vocal intonation in the Arabic. "Thank you for your initiative that is killing us. We thank our brothers in Sahnaya and Al-Ashrafiya (sarcasm) for your 'humanitarian work' that is preventing us from getting even medicine and from [sic] preventing us from treating our wounded. Thanks a lot. (sarcasm)." Scrolling through the page, the posts consist largely of cell phone images of children in their shrouds, children lying on the ground with their faces covered in blood, children screaming and crying as blood gushes from their noses and eyes. It's absolutely brutal to bear.

As is typical on Facebook, each image is accompanied by a caption or posting (positioned usually before the picture as one scrolls down, and comments are at the bottom). Many such posts appeal to the rhetoric of identification, saying, for example, "This little boy you are seeing could be my child, or your cousin, or even tour [sic] neighbor, his name is AbdulRahman Al Dakheel, he's 7 years old. He was in second grade. AbdulRahmad [sic] was martyred three days ago. . . . She [sic] wasn't in a refugee camp, he wasn't in a shelter, he wasn't at a protest, HE WAS AT HIS HOUSE, PLAYING LIKE ANY CHILD IN THIS WORLD" (June 30, 2012). Here the plea to identification is explicit—this could be your child, my child, your neighbor. The innocence of childhood is underlined by the assertion that this child died in his home, while playing, and not in a place where he might have been at risk or accidentally caught in the line of fire.

Other posts make particular reference to the practice of sharing horrific images by connecting it to the indifference of the world political community and to the need for ordinary citizens worldwide to help Syria. This post appears above an image of two young children in their coffins, decked in flowers: "We are sorry that we keep on bringing sad pictures and videos to you, but this is Syria now, we know that you must feel the same, but we need to share this you and the world. . . . We know that we only have people to our side, and not governments, so from one human to another, please share and help us, let the world hear our screams." As with the original video, the act of seeing is framed itself a witnessing act that comes with the obligation to "share," to spread the images further.

It is impossible to judge what the impact of this site may have in a situation that is ongoing as of this writing and very much in flux. My interest here is not to adjudicate the usefulness or efficacy of these images, or social activism via networking sites like Facebook and Twitter (which, as I mentioned earlier, have been a big part of the Western news discussion of the Arab Spring). What can be explored here is the ways in which images of one particular corpse came to operate as the shadow text behind such a display. The purpose of such an exploration is to theorize what happens to that very material trace once it's taken up in this context.

Specifically, what is the dynamic between the named corpse of Hamza al-Khateeb and the relatively anonymous bodies shown on the Facebook page, under the auspices of his "about to die" face? Remember that every post appears with the icon bearing his profile picture in a thumbnail next to it; the site is also written in the first person singular, as though al-Khateeb were himself looking down, commenting, calling on our sense of mercy, responsibility, outrage. Although there are post-ings about press coverage, and less often about political events, such as the defection of a high-level general of the Syrian army, the site func-tions mostly to share images that rival the al-Khateeb autopsy video in graphic horror. And while many of them are named and the places and circumstances of their deaths may be given, the corpses displayed in the name of Hamza al-Khateeb are decontextualized. They scroll past as a gallery of horrors, and even the toughest viewer would arguably have trouble stopping to read the names and details of each death, of each corpse on display. I'm probably a good example for this, as I've been doing months of research on the site; I feel viscerally, physically ill when I spend more than a few moments looking at it, and I find that in moments when I'm not researching, I actively ignore the posts from "We Are ALL Hamza al-Khateeb" that appear in my newsfeed, because I am simply not able to bear it at that moment. Again, though this may point to critiques like Sontag's call for an "ecology of images,"[58] the point is that although I know a great deal about al-Khateeb, the bodies displayed under his auspices online are decontextualized, anonymous. They are more object than subject; closer to flesh than to personhood, they are atrocity, not tragedy.

Al-Khateeb's death is legible as metaphor—as simultaneously simi-lar to and different from the boy who was killed. The Facebook page explicitly figures the corpse as both al-Khateeb *and* anyone else. "We are all Hamza al-Khateeb" is a metaphor that links the likeness of the proper name—the referential, indexical quality of remains—to the otherness of remaining, of no longer referring solely to the departed.

DISRUPTIVE IMAGES, MOMENTS OF
DOMESTICATION, AND RESISTANCE

Two moments in the circulation of these photographic relics of mar-tyred bodies are of interest in showing how these images, or eruptive encounters, resist domestication in a linear narrative of social change. The first is the juxtaposition, both in *Jet* and at the funeral, of the corpse of Emmett Till with a photograph of him in life. In the photograph, taken the Christmas before his death, Till leans against a large televi-sion set in the living room of his Chicago apartment. The television as a literal emblem for mediated representation also signifies as a class marker—a luxury consumer good emblematic of the advances the Great Migration had supposedly conferred on northern blacks. Outside of the original publication context, within a network of black magazines and newspapers that helped forge the solidarity that would support the civil rights movement, this juxtaposition is most often lost. We only see the bloated corpse, the famous image almost unrecognizable as human and certainly bearing no resemblance to the smiling boy in the other photograph. This juxtaposition decontextualizes the eruption of the violence in the photographic relic and allows it to be sidelined in the history of the civil rights movement, and thus in ongoing discussions of racial violence in the United States, which the Till image, out of context, suggests is a relic of some barbarous past and not a reality happening all over the country.

The second moment is in the YouTube video showing the corpse of Hamza al-Khateeb, and it is the fact of the pixelation of the genitals of the corpse, captioned with the statement, "YouTube does not allow explicit images." As if nothing in the video before then—the bullet holes, the dead boy's bruised face, the shattered kneecaps—had been explicit! The activists who made the video filmed the genitals because they wanted to prove that the boy had been castrated. In the accompanying narration (subtitled in English), the castration is the most heinous crime and the clearest marker of torture and barbarism. To castrate this boy is to attack his humanity in the cruelest and most humiliating way. That YouTube, which is owned by Google, should deem this detail and no other "explicit" enough to pixelate thus blunts the video's most forceful claim on the imagination and outrage of its viewers. I am not saying that without this detail the video is ineffective or that it does not, even in its censored form, spark outrage, horror, and pity. But that little spot of blindness and distortion is the trace of the global economy on that suffering, an attempt to domesticate and narrativize its affective claims at their most poignant. It is precisely where the violence moves beyond the *body* of Hamza al-Khateeb and into his *personhood* where our gaze is censored. Though this arguably protects al-Khateeb's dignity and personhood, it is a direct countermove to the intentions of the activists who made the video, with the permission of al-Khateeb's parents.

Images of Atrocity

Images of atrocity are spectacular failures when it comes to preventing further violence. The Argentine human rights slogan *Nunca mas!* (Never again!) grates mournfully against the sensibilities of a viewer who has watched it happen again, and again, and again—in Rwanda, in Bosnia, in Syria. "This time, we knew," writes Sharon Sliwinski of the legalistic contempt of images in discussions of human rights. She argues that an abandonment of aesthetic analysis of these images abdicates the real potential, though unrealized, for encountering distant others.[59]

Rather than asking how these videos and other images failed to mobilize adequate political action—a question that leads to either a condemnation or justification of the image—I turn to the question of how they become legible. What are the ramifications of the contingent and specific deployment of this material object, this corpse? What work is the corpse itself doing to organize and propel the appeal to help the people of Syria—when it is visible, or when it operates only as a kind of shadow text captioning other images? Given the corpse's complex representational dynamics, how does this particular corpse appear as meaningful matter?

Asking these questions implies an interest in the particular body of Hamza al-Khateeb, which, despite its specific materiality, becomes also a metaphor for the plight of the Syrian people. It entails attention to how this particular body might exceed its reference to one person. I am interested in the cultural processes that suture the material existence of *this body* and its suffering to broader notions of injustice and identification. Some interplay between the particular and the universal makes the phrase "we are *all* Hamza al-Khateeb" legible—even in English, to Western Facebook users. What of the corpse itself is made visible or legible or meaningful in that phrase, and what of the corpse is effaced therein?

This example opens the corpse's vexed ontology onto the question of human rights and political agency. The following chapter analyzes how the corpse of Michael Jackson became a figure in a broader discussion about the relationship between race and appearance. Nevertheless, Jackson himself was a pop culture figure, an entertainer whose personal political ambitions were only attributed posthumously. One might very well say the same of al-Khateeb—but his corpse becomes significant in a vastly different context. Al-Khateeb's corpse is charged with meaning because he was a young, unknown, ordinary boy before he died—and because that ordinary life was so violently and abhorrently cut off. Hamza al-Khateeb was not a celebrity in life.

Emmett Till's corpse said the unsayable, made abject horror real for all those who attended the memorial or saw the images in print.[60] Both the corpse and the photographs are strongly indexical: they bear witness to racial violence as something irrefutably real. The marks on the body are themselves indices of torture; the photographic image adds a layer to this representational strategy by allowing the corpse to circulate beyond the limits of its material duration. In both cases, the world-making imperative of testimony is shouldered not linguistically but by a signifying object: a corpse, a photograph.

This hypervisual corpse asserts itself into public life through the representational strategies described here in a way that is different from traditional mourning. It remains as a relic of racial violence and thus a reminder, a challenge, to those who might want to forget or forgive such occurrences. In this way, the corpse of Emmett Till cannot be buried but must remain a visible remainder, a relic that creates a kind of communal melancholia. So long as the goals of the civil rights movement remain unmet, Till's corpse cannot be buried, cannot disappear.

In contrast, the corpses of what I am calling *tabloid bodies* in the next chapter are conspicuously invisible in the context of a public life that was almost constantly in view. These corpses, of Diana, Princess of Wales, and of Michael Jackson, are abject without the recuperation found in the identification with Till and Hamza al-Khateeb. Instead, the corpse is ritually expelled from the regime of images so as to maintain the archive of images of life as not only sealed but endlessly productive. These are corpses without bodies, a true realm of the living dead.

3

TABLOID BODIES
Princess Diana and Michael Jackson

This chapter examines the live television memorials of Michael Jackson and Diana, Princess of Wales, with particular focus on the eulogies that "captioned" the televisual presence of the casket. In this corpus, which I am calling *tabloid bodies,* the corpses of the King of Pop and the People's Princess are spots of invisibility in their otherwise hypervisual lives and legacies. Their legacies involve the ongoing commodification of their bodies and of their children's bodies, which requires that the corpse itself be expelled as abject.

Tabloid bodies combine the visibility of the martyr's body with the renown of the king. Famous in life, tabloid bodies die early and scandalous deaths. In the tabloid body, a hypervisual living body often results in an invisible or concealed corpse. Mourning these deaths implicates the strange intimacy of the parasocial as visual media memorialize in pictures and moving images a person who is beloved without being known. In this sense, tabloid bodies bring together all of our themes of the nation and belonging, of martyrdom and distant suffering, of media and materialism. In the tabloid gaze, their deaths are chiaroscuro portraits of modern melancholy.

I mean a few different things when I say the corpses are conspicuously absent, each of which is significant here. First of all, photographs of their corpses exist but have not circulated. Their corpses were photographed because they were tabloid figures: pictures of them, any pictures, but particularly those depicting scandal or embarrassment, sold papers. Paparazzi were present at the scene of Diana's accident and continued photographing the scene even after the crash.[1] Photographs taken at the crash were shown as evidence in the inquest into Diana's death, but unlike all the other evidence introduced, they were not published.[2] A photograph of Michael Jackson's corpse, lying naked on a hospital gurney, was also introduced as part of the forensic report in the manslaughter trial of his doctor, Conrad Murray.[3] These official photographs, both of which fall into the category of evidence in a court of law, are not part of the enormous visual archives of these very public lives.[4]

More to the point here, however, is the conspicuous absence of the corpse in both funerals, which were broadcast live. The particular combination of the image of the casket and the presence effect of televisual liveness makes the corpse an absent presence in a powerful way.[5] Diana's funeral broadcast included footage of the casket's transport from the palace to Westminster Abbey, as crowds paid their respects along the way. One of the funeral's unforgettable details is that on the front of the casket was a card reading simply "Mummy" in a child's hand. Without seeing the corpse itself, then, we have an indelible image of the casket, itself an indexical referent to the remains inside.

Michael Jackson's casket was also part of the live broadcast, borne into the Staples Center by his brothers and placed in front of the stage, where it was in the foreground of every shot. Some performers even addressed the casket in their tributes, as, for example, when the singer Usher actually touched the casket, visibly moved, during his performance of the song "Gone Too Soon." Here, too, the casket was a conspicuous visual marker for the hidden remains. It echoed the "Liberace goes to war" aesthetic of Jackson's performance costumes: huge, plated in shining fourteen karat gold, and crowned with an enormous funeral flower arrangement in red and white.[6] This prominence of the casket in both memorials is what made the corpse an absent presence. Its reality was not visual but indexical, relying both on the liveness of the broadcast and on the casket as a signifier of what remains unseen. In its reference to the unseen body, the live image of each casket also discursively delineated the social identity of the deceased—in Diana's case, of a populist princess who was nevertheless the virgin mother of kings, and in Jackson's case, of a black pop icon whose ethnic belonging transcended race as a visual signifier.

TABLOID MARTYRDOM: LEGACY AS COMMODITY FETISH

Michael Jackson and Diana, Princess of Wales, were the biggest tabloid stars of the 1980s and 1990s. Both enjoyed global fame and lived under almost constant photographic scrutiny, which led to disordered or dysmorphic relations to embodiment. For Diana, this was her confessed struggle with bulimia; Jackson did not speak publicly about his plastic surgeries, but they were widely read as pathological. They both raised children in relationship to this intense visibility, and these children represent, for both Jackson and Diana, a public legacy.

How does the corpse of a tabloid body mean as matter? By remaining the one spot of invisibility in a hypervisible afterlife. Photographs of both corpses are conspicuously absent from the image archive of their memory—an archive that continues to function as a living assemblage, churning out memorial concerts and posthumous albums and never-before-seen images. Writing at the time of Diana's death, Adrien Kear describes a "ritual economy of postmodern mediatization" in which Diana is "seemingly always-already entombed" within the economy of the image. After her death, "without the restriction of a living referent, these industries of reverence, revenance and remembrance were no longer held back by the demands of ontological presence."[7] In the years since Diana's death, the "demands of ontological presence" have proved even more irrelevant to a long and lucrative afterlife. Diana appeared on the cover of *Vanity Fair* in 2014, sixteen years after her death, as the world awaited the birth of her first grandchild;[8] more controversially, in 2011, *Newsweek*'s cover used a digitally enhanced photograph of Diana to imagine what she might look like at fifty.[9] Jackson powers his own industry of remembrance: eight studio albums of previously unreleased tracks are scheduled for posthumous release; at the 2014 Billboard Music Awards, Epic Records produced a holographic performance by Michael Jackson, using new technology to blend archival video footage, live musicians, and choreography.[10] These vivid afterlives preclude images of death in their technologically enhanced quest to keep their images alive as commodities and brands.

Jackson and Diana had their last appearance in the flesh at their funerals, both of which were broadcast live on television. These "media events"[11] are what Paul Frosh has called a "witnessing text," where an effect of presence is produced in the interaction between audience and text. As memorials, the live broadcasts engaged a "witnessing modality," that is, a sense that engagement with the world the text creates (the life whose passing is mourned) is morally important.[12] How does the witnessing text of the televisual memorial *assemble a corpus* that calls upon our grief as morally important?

The eulogies delivered at the live memorials transformed tabloid scandal into a kind of pop martyrdom by focusing on their humanitarian activities. In this narrative, fame becomes a burden that Diana and Jackson bore for the sake of others—to make visible the plight of distant others. The highly visible humanitarianism of a figure like Bono or Angelina Jolie has its precursor in the spectacle of Diana cradling a child infected with HIV or in Jackson's "Man in the Mirror" video, which featured images of the famine in Ethiopia as part of his Heal the World Foundation's humanitarian efforts.[13] In death, this humanitarianism provides the impetus to a narrative that rewrites their scandals and eccentricities as the price of fame and the humanitarian causes as the elevating martyrdom that makes our witnessing of their passing morally important.

In this assemblage, affect and the image combine to make a selectively political portrait of a life whose economic value is maintained by the continued circulation of archival media. In other words, in observing their passing as morally important, we are also sanctioned to consume their public image as a way to partake in and carry forward their humanitarian goals. For this to work, the corpse must remain absent as visual signifier in the moment of passing. In both memorials it appears in the casket, but the image of death as the image of the deceased himself or herself is not part of this corpus. Thus Diana and Michael Jackson may be continually sought and resurrected in the sites of their disappearance: the site of tabloid fame and celebrity gossip becomes also a space of redemption.

This is legacy as commodity fetish, as a material object—a magazine cover, a posthumous album, the image of a royal grandchild—that conceals, in its mute physicality, the dynamic relations of social reproduction out of which it emerges. Insofar as death is one of these relations, it too is subject to this fetishization. Insofar as we consume tabloid bodies via archival media, the material truth of their corpses must be disavowed.

"DON'T FOCUS ON THE SCARS, FOCUS ON THE JOURNEY": REDEEMING THE IMAGE

Michael Jackson and Diana of Wales were constantly photographed for most of their adult lives, both of which coincided with the rise of tabloid culture and paparazzi photography.[14] Whatever their accomplishments may have been, their bodies as visible objects were always news—fodder for speculation and admiration.

The corpse has a special role in constructing the witnessing modality of Diana's and Michael Jackson's memorials in that it is part of what "creates presence at the event" and "produces experience out of discourse."[15] In particular—as a semiotic element in a text that is also a signifier of materiality itself—the corpse worked as part of the larger text of the memorial to regulate and reframe the alternative testimonies of the photographs of these controversial and highly visual figures. The corpse becomes the absent presence that stands for the invisible *something* transforming a tabloid body into a martyr to fame.

In each memorial, audiences not only bore witness to death but found it materially present in the corpse itself. That is, there was a casket at each memorial—though at neither was it opened. Not only did this give the memorials the immediacy and intimacy of an actual funeral (as opposed to a more distant retrospective), it also highlighted the indexicality of live television. The casket affirms that what is happening before the lens is specific in space and time. Without the casket, the memorial could be anywhere or anytime: with so many photographs and so much video to draw on for both of these figures, their deaths and lives both take place for most of us in the circular time and uncertain space of their vast archive of media, Kittler's realm of the dead. Instead, the presence of the casket grounds the memorial. The corpse to which it attests is in some sense an auratic object, existing only in a particular time and place and no other. So, too, the memorial feels auratic, even as millions witness at a distance.

I'll be looking at two specific moments, one from each memorial, to show how these tabloid bodies form part of an assemblage that depends, crucially, on their *invisible* presence. The continued legacies of these tabloid bodies depend on this invisibility because it is a commercial legacy. The Jackson estate has paid off its $30 million in debt; with William and Katherine's wedding and the births of Prince George and Princess Charlotte, the British monarchy is arguably more popular than ever. Death has played an important role in this by dignifying posthumous fame with moral significance. Both eulogies—the first by Diana's brother, the Earl of Spencer, and the second by the Reverend Al Sharpton—contextualize death as part of a larger narrative arc in which fame and its accessory, the image, are recast as sacrifices made to a higher moral cause. In the case of Diana, that cause is the reform of the monarchy and the quest to raise a "normal" family within its confines; in the case of Michael Jackson, that cause is racial equality in the United States as epitomized by the election of Barack Obama as president.

The live image of the corpse signifies death, while its invisibility allows other images to take its place, images that contribute to the on-going monetization and commodification of the deceased's memory. If the images of Emmett Till and Hamza al-Khateeb were relics of modern martyrs, images of Princess Diana and Michael Jackson are fetishes, objects that disavow the fact of their deaths. These corpses cannot mean as matter: we do not mourn them, because we must continue to consume them, and for us to consume them, they must remain continually productive. They cannot, in other words, decompose and disappear.

The invisibility of the corpses themselves is a condition of their afterlives as commodity fetishes. The public image of their deaths is not of a corpse but a shared image of the casket at a live memorial and a narrative about the price of fame. These invisible bodies underwrite the posthumous production of images, images that, with the recaptioning provided by the eulogies, are cleansed of their association with excess, decadence, and scandal.

Earl Spencer's Eulogy for Diana

Diana's brother, the Earl Spencer's eulogy framed her death as "part of a religious cycle of sin and redemption, a genuinely good and Christian woman who was martyred for our sins."[16] On the morning after her death, speaking from his home in Cape Town, South Africa, the Earl said, "I always believed the press would kill her in the end."[17] The rhetoric of his eulogy works to separate the notion of Diana's "extraordinary appeal" from her fame and visibility. Her "magic" and her "appeal" are essential, invisible—while those who hunted her for her image only saw the surface appeal. This critique of the press is symbolically elided with a condemnation of the royal family, which had revoked her royal title ("HRH") after her divorce and whose stuffiness and rigid protocol were seen as contributing to Diana's unhappiness in life. Spencer emphasizes that Diana had no need of titles to "generate her particular brand of magic," once again drawing a distinction between surface characteristics, the accidentals of beauty and title, and the truth of essence:

> For such was her extraordinary appeal that the tens of millions of people taking part in this service all over the world via television and radio who never actually met her, feel that they too lost someone close to them in the early hours of Sunday morning. It is a more remarkable tribute to Diana than I can ever hope to offer her today.
>
> Diana was the very essence of compassion, of duty, of style, of beauty. All over the world she was a symbol of selfless humanity. All over the world, a standard bearer for the rights of the truly downtrodden, a very British girl who transcended nationality. Someone with a natural nobility who was classless and who proved in the last year that she needed no royal title to continue to generate her particular brand of magic.[18]

The rhetoric here is remarkably complex, all the more so because reading it with the benefit of the thirteen intervening years one can instantly see to what extent this eulogy has crystallized as the image of Diana, indeed, her branding within the larger commodification of the royal family—a British girl turned princess who earned the love of people worldwide by championing the very lowest among them. Though inextricable from a particular national context, Diana belongs to us all now—indeed, she can continue her work as a "symbol of selfless humanity" without effort, unencumbered by the trials of the flesh. Her work as "symbol," however, is not visual—it is not her beauty or popularity or any other external characteristic that makes her special. As the Earl shifts into the second person to directly address Diana, he reinforces the line between invisible essence and external glamour. This distinction allows him to locate Diana's highly visible and public life within a narrative of sacrifice and redemption:

But your greatest gift was your intuition and it was a gift you used wisely. This is what underpinned all your other wonderful attributes and if we look to analyze what it was about you that had such a wide appeal we find it in your instinctive feel for what was really important in all our lives.

Without your God-given sensitivity we would be immersed in greater ignorance at the anguish of AIDS and HIV sufferers, the plight of the homeless, the isolation of lepers, the random destruction of land mines.

Diana explained to me once that it was her innermost feelings of suffering that made it possible for her to connect with her constituency of the rejected. And here we come to another truth about her. For all the status, the glamour, the applause, Diana remained throughout a very insecure person at heart, almost childlike in her desire to do good for others so she could release herself from deep feelings of unworthiness of which her eating disorders were merely a symptom.

The world sensed this part of her character and cherished her for her vulnerability whilst admiring her for her honesty.[19]

This is a long quotation, but I haven't abridged it because each of the moves is so crucial to see here. We've already seen how a second person address moves the attention away from the body itself and back to the memory of the deceased. In speaking directly to his sister, the Earl rhetorically invokes her memory and gives it life, so that when he's giving her attributes like "God-given sensitivity" or "instinctive feel for what was important in all of our lives" or "deep feelings of unworthiness," he creates her, his words part of the assemblage holding Diana together with her image, her body, and her memory.

Here again, glamour and status are compared unfavorably as mere surface distractions, while the essence of Diana was in her "innermost feelings of suffering." These feelings are themselves invisible but make themselves manifest in greater visibility for others: the ravaged bodies of people with HIV, of lepers, of victims of land mines. Diana's "constituency of the rejected" is literally brought to light via the invisible suffering of her beautiful body, a suffering "of which her eating disorders were merely a symptom." Surface symptom versus God-given insight: the truth of Diana is in the casket and in the liveness that makes it present to the world, but not in the body itself. It is ethereal, noncorporeal—which is why it is so easily communicable. In signifying the "visibility of the hidden," the casket allows the corpse to mean as matter only insofar as it is out of sight.

FIGURE 12. Casket of Diana, Princess of Wales, with a rose bouquet and the note reading "Mummy" in the foreground. Getty Images/Anwar Hussein.

If Earl Spencer's eulogy crystallizes Diana's legacy, it is perhaps because of the reaction it drew. The memorial took place inside Westminster Abbey, but in addition to the millions watching on television, an enormous crowd outside the abbey, on the streets, were able to hear the eulogy via loudspeakers. Beginning with the comment about how Diana "needed no royal titles to generate her particular brand of magic," the crowd outside began to applaud. The applause was the perfect symbol of Diana's popular acclaim: in violation of royal decorum, they turned the funeral into a performance and expressed their approval in a raucous and intrusive manner. The sound of the applause was loud enough to penetrate the abbey. When Earl Spencer finished speaking, the people inside the abbey applauded as well. It was a stunningly powerful moment of consensus: by applauding him despite the demands of polite conduct and funerary decorum, the privileged spectators inside the abbey expressed their solidarity with the "constituency of the rejected" whose presence had burst into their confines. For that moment, the hierarchy of presence was reversed, and those who witnessed at a distance had a privileged emotional relationship to the deceased.

That incident, along with Elton John's adaptation of his song "Candle in the Wind," originally written about Marilyn Monroe, as "Goodbye England's Rose" in tribute to Diana, formed the crucible of the popular understanding of Diana's death being in some way "about" monarchy, tradition, fame, and publicity. Mourning Diana "depended upon a life which was colossally, excessively, represented. This was a life in which sexual relations 'in private' were often public, in which death itself was in, or by, the camera's eye."[20] The involvement of paparazzi photographers in her death and their eventual trial (and acquittal) meant that mourning was also in the public eye. Popular sentiment erupted in the closed space of the memorial, inverting the traditional distinctions between the auratic, live presence and the televisual representation of the same.

Reverend Al Sharpton's Eulogy for Michael Jackson

Unlike Diana's, who had to confess to secrets like her bulimia or her infidelity, Jackson's scars were all too visible, as "plain as the nose on his face."[21] Tabloid coverage of Jackson's bizarre behavior and, in particular, his plastic surgeries had earned him the nickname "Wacko Jacko."[22] The armchair psychological interpretation of these surgeries was racialized self-hatred—Jackson's abusive father had criticized his appearance, calling him "fat nose" and "lubber lips." This racialized shaming and abuse, combined with a childhood spent in the public eye, had rendered Jackson a plastic surgery addict, a "Peter Pan" who could not grow up, and perhaps even a pedophile. As Nikki Sullivan incisively illustrates, there is a politics to this reading of Jackson's body: an assumption of a homogenous and interpretable self that is distinguishable from, rather than produced in concert with, the modificatory practices that shape it.[23] In tabloid coverage as well as documentaries like *Michael Jackson: The Face,* Jackson's face becomes a "fleshly confession of his inner turmoil" and even an augury of his coming self-destruction.

In the memorialization of Michael Jackson, these apparent acts of self-hatred are recast as stigmata. Crucially, however, this rereading of "the face" does not question any of the basic assumptions about the body as a text that tells the truth of a homogenous and interpretable subjectivity within. Rather, the elements are rearranged so that Jackson's blackness becomes an essential and a crucially nonvisual entity that persists despite his bodily modifications. No matter what color his skin or what shape his nose, the visibility of this *essentially* black body is what allows for racial change. Jackson's blackness becomes not a visual signifier that his surgeries mutilate but instead an essential inner quality informing every aspect of his public life.

Borne by Jackson's brothers, the casket entered from the back of the Staples Center, while on-stage a gospel choir sang. It was then placed just in front of the stage so that any long or even medium long shot of the stage could not fail to include it. Unlike Diana's memorial, which was shot from the perspective of a single camera at a time, Jackson's memorial also featured "reaction shots" of the Jackson family and others in the audience. These shots, which indicated the use of several cameras and on-the-fly editing, always showed the casket as the shot shifted from the podium to the larger space of the Staples Center. This visual marker of his corpse's invisibility was the focus point, drawing the eye with its gleaming gold plate and enormous crown of red roses—a casket fit for the King of Pop.

As a signifier of materiality itself (and thus the resistance of matter

to representation), the corpse also offered an alternative mode of witnessing than the photograph's perilously misleading indexicality. The
television audience was thus called on to witness Jackson's life as symbolized by his body. In so doing, it also bore witness to the redemption
of the material as a means of signification adequate to the gravity of
the situation.

This redemption of Jackson's body as a signifier of an appropriately decorous legacy was discursively produced by the eulogy of the
Reverend Al Sharpton. Speaking with the flower-decked casket almost
always in the foreground of the shot, Sharpton's rhetoric and imagery
reframed the body as the vehicle for a larger, more important project
of racial integration:

> When Michael started, it was a different world, but . . . [he] broke
> down the color curtain, when now our videos are shown and maga-
> zines put us on the cover; it was Michael Jackson that brought blacks
> and whites and Asians and Latinos together! . . . Young kids grew up
> from being teenage comfortable fans of Michael to being forty years
> old and being comfortable to vote for a person of color to be the
> President of the United States of America. Michael did that, Michael
> made us love each other, Michael taught us to stand with each other.[24]

Michael Jackson's visibility as a performer is directly linked to the
comfort level to which Sharpton refers and thus is in no way troubled
by his changing skin color and appearance. Rather, those elements of
the visual archive are condensed in the physical personhood of Michael
Jackson, in a body that "broke down the color curtain"—culminating in
the election of a biracial president who himself symbolizes the healing
of racial divisions in the political body of the nation.

Sharpton continued, recuperating Jackson's mutilated body for a
higher purpose, transforming his scars into stigmata:

> There are those that like to dig around mess, but . . . it's not about
> mess, it's about his love message. As you climb up steep mountains,
> sometime you scar your knee, sometime you break your skin, but
> don't focus on the scars, focus on the journey!

Rather than dwelling in the ambiguity of his performance of race and
gender, Sharpton converts Jackson's "radical heteromorphism"[25] into
teleology, his scars into stigmata. The internal rhyme between "mess"

and "love *message*" inscribes the homogeneity that we simply *could not see* because it was not a matter of seeing but a matter of hearing. Jackson's legacy is not his face but his voice.

As with Earl Spencer's eulogy, Sharpton's rhetoric urges us to remember an unseen essential quality irreducible to the enormous (tabloid) photographic archive. If in Diana's case the point was to extricate her "appeal" from her visibility by locating it in an ethereal compassion, Sharpton asks us not to believe our eyes but rather Jackson's words (to garble a Groucho Marx quote oft exploited by Slavoj Žižek to describe the fetish). This message had particular potency in the context of the days following Jackson's death, when MTV and other twenty-four-hour cable outlets were an endless slideshow shuffling randomly from era to era of Jackson's life: the adorable kid with an Afro and a shy smile; the diamond-gloved King of Pop; the pale, bewigged eccentric with the ruined nose. Sharpton's eulogy helped make a new story out of these conflicting images, wherein the meaning of Jackson's life was to be found elsewhere than in the often-disturbing appearances. What we saw or thought we saw was not the truth at all. We were not watching a man who hated himself or his gender or his ethnicity—we were not watching a mess. We were hearing a love message.

Sharpton's rhetoric is complicated by the fact that he locates the efficacy of that message of racial harmony in Jackson's visibility. Whereas Diana's gift was to make the "constituency of the rejected" visible through her innate understanding, Jackson's gift is also an internal essence. His blackness here is an essence that translates into visual comfort with other black bodies on-screen. "Now our videos are shown," and "now magazines put us on their covers"—these were barriers that Jackson broke that are meaningless except in terms of a politics of visibility. This rhetoric echoes a common conception that Jackson's meaningful achievements are restricted to the era "when he was black"[26]—meaning both when he looked African American in terms of skin color and when his music and style were most heavily associated with black street culture. The Jackson Five recorded with Motown; Jackson first did the moonwalk at a Motown retrospective concert. His dancing style and fashion sense drew on the break-dance culture on the streets and subways of New York. Jackson's "Billie Jean" was the first video by an African American artist played in heavy rotation on MTV,[27] making

Jackson a global pop icon in a very visual moment. Sharpton draws on this aspect of his superstardom to make the claim that without Michael Jackson, there would be no Barack Obama: it is the literal comfort that comes with seeing black faces on TV all day, every day from a young age, as the MTV generation did, to which Sharpton attributes the social changes that would eventually elect Obama. If Jackson's blackness eventually became invisible or ambiguous, it is irrelevant to the fact of his essential blackness, one that goes deeper than skin color.

As Sharpton says, the question is one of focus. We have a visual record that does not tell the whole truth of Jackson's "love message"—conversely, the efficacy of that "love message" depended not only on Jackson's visibility but also on a racially coded visibility, one that read clearly as African American. When he says "don't focus on the scars, focus on the journey," he locates the truth of Jackson's contributions to the cause of racial equality in the fullness of time rather than on the surface of the skin. The kind of seeing that matters, in Sharpton's rhetoric, is the kind that sees past the surface.

With Sharpton's deep focus, Jackson's self-mutilations become stigmata. The "high mountains" that Jackson climbed—the obstacles of racism and discrimination, even, Sharpton implies, of culturally conditioned self-hatred—are the cause of his scraped knees and scarred skin. Jackson is a martyr in the sense that the visibility of fame scarred and eventually killed him:

> And I want his three children to know: wasn't nothing strange about your daddy; it was strange what your daddy had to deal with; but he dealt with it [applause, almost thirty seconds] . . . he dealt with it anyway, he dealt with it for us!

Sharpton addresses the children as a way of invoking the future: it is they who will carry forward their father's memory, and it is Sharpton's job to set the record straight, to let them know their father wasn't "strange." Sharpton rhetorically demolishes the image of "Wacko Jacko" with an indictment of the culture that produced that image. Jackson's face here is still a map of suffering, and even perversion, but the perversion is cultural, and the suffering is redemptive.

As my transcript shows, this portion of Sharpton's comments drew lengthy applause from the audience. It didn't seem out of place at

Michael Jackson's memorial, which was so much more like a concert than a funeral, complete with the gleaming rock star casket in front of the stage. In the nearly fifteen years between the deaths of these two colossal tabloid figures, the narrative of the martyr to fame has been fleshed out, furnished with its own set of observances.

The enduring interpretation of Diana's martyrdom has not been for the sins of the tabloid press but for the sins of the British royalty. Writing at the time of her death, Kear and Steinberg observed that "for one royalist section of pro-Diana opinion, she came to represent not what promise was offered first through herself, by performance as much as vows, but a promise was also made through or on behalf of her children, in her own lived fantasy of William as a 'once and future king' of a new kind. To another kind of pro-Diana sentiment, her life and struggles showed up the oppressive roles of royalty, strengthening a preference for republican solutions."[28] The intervening years have upheld the former promise—of a new kind of "once and future king." We have a modern, down-to-earth monarchy, offering a certain kind of accessibility in exchange for control of its public image.[29]

LIVING LEGACIES

When we consider their children, the theme of visibility and invisibility in the corpus of Diana and Michael Jackson grows poignant. Their parents are absolved of the photograph: their martyrdom constructs their legacies as essence rather than appearance. As living legacies, the children are still subject to photographic scrutiny and will themselves take up the mantle of fame and its attendant visibility.

In both cases, this is a problematic inheritance. Diana's confessed infidelities have led to questions about the paternity of her son Harry, who some say bears a close resemblance to one of her lovers. No one will ever force Harry to take a DNA test, and indeed one of the privileges of actual royalty is that this kind of speculation can only go so far before propriety cuts it off. But his body becomes an object of scrutiny in the public gaze. Why doesn't Harry share the same balding pattern Charles obviously passed on to William? If he marries and has children, will any of the classic Windsor features make an appearance? As the second son (the "spare"), Harry's public role is less formal. His behavior seems to match this: it was he, not first son William, who was photographed in Las Vegas playing pool in the nude, and it was he who was photographed at Halloween dressed in an SS officer's costume. His body is the tabloid site, the site of scandal and uncertain paternity—in the sense Derrida has given the term, that is, of proper meaning as well as biological provenance—that still haunts the royal family. If Diana's body is abject, then Harry's is the return of the repressed.

William's body is more complex. He is already "performing" his paternity, with the same bald patch and slightly stiff demeanor of his father and his mother's fair hair and blue eyes. William is where Diana's sacrifice finds its redemption: it is he who will be a down-to-earth royal who will, as much as his role allows, lead as much of a "normal" life as possible. These phrases, particularly the odd notion of a normal life, again find their origin in Earl Spencer's eulogy:

> And beyond that, on behalf of your mother and sisters, I pledge that we, your blood family, will do all we can to continue the imaginative and loving way in which you were steering these two exceptional young men so that their souls are not simply immersed by duty and tradition, but can sing openly as you planned.[30]

What is a "normal" life, and how does it produce a soul able to "sing openly"? Much was made in Diana's lifetime of her casual, hands-on parenting style. Her performance of motherhood was often in open defiance of the stiff, restrained, and distantly formal style associated with the tradition of the British monarchy—one that, as Earl Spencer notes, emphasizes duty above all. There are many photographs of Diana holding her children, playing and laughing with them—which was at the time unusual in comparison to the formal portraits of Charles and his siblings as children. The children's card on the casket was a visual cue, amid traditional ritual elements, that Diana was a particular kind of mother, a "regular mom" to her sons. That Diana was in some way prevented from exercising this "natural" role by the strictness of royal protocol is read as one of the central tragedies of her death. Hence Earl Spencer's pledge to steer the young princes' souls toward open song rather than the kind of festering repression that has become the popular reading of the failure of Charles and Diana's marriage, as well as Queen Elizabeth's failure to respond with adequate emotion to the news of Diana's death, as depicted in the popular film *The Queen.*

Whether or not these things are true, they are now firmly entrenched as popular mythology and armchair psychology: Charles denied himself his first and true love, Camilla, and ended up disgracing himself and his marriage by being unfaithful with her anyway (Charles and Camilla's eventual marriage and her relatively easy integration into the current life of the royal family can be read as a kind of reparative gesture, with the public largely understanding that this is "how things should be"). Diana's natural exuberance and youth were squelched by the strict demands of her public role: she developed bulimia, attempted suicide, and, as the world's most "hunted" figure, was eventually driven to death.

This is not only the story as the public remembers it and as it is told in tabloids and biographies. It is also the story that the royals themselves act out through the symbolism of their public behavior. They cannot now be unaware of the "branding crisis" the royalty went through after Diana's death. Strategic breaks with protocol that gesture toward a "normal" life as the overdetermined signifier of goodness and mental health have been, for example, the hallmark of William's courtship, marriage, and now parenthood. Unlike Diana and Charles, who barely knew each other before becoming engaged, William and Katherine dated for eight years and even lived together before they married, in contrast to Diana's much vaunted virginity. Since the birth of their children, Katherine and William both are often photographed actively parenting, as, for example, during their official tour of New Zealand and Australia in spring 2014, where baby Prince George took center stage. This performance of "normal" coupledom and parent-hood reassures the public—who are, of course, the consumers of their brand—that Diana's sacrifice was not in vain.[31] This will be the fairy tale that they had hoped for Diana, but a modern, realistic fairy tale, where the prince and princess shop off the rack and change diapers. Meanwhile, Katherine wears Diana's signature sapphire and diamond engagement ring and dresses in ways deliberately designed to evoke her mother-in-law's fashion sense and glamour. It's very suited to our age of celebrity accessibility and to the way that fame—and, crucially, its attendant visibility—is now parceled out as if it were an inalienable right. The royals are just like us, except when they aren't.[32]

If Diana's children have become more visible as they have grown older and have worked to perform their mother's legacy, Michael Jackson's children have appeared in the public eye in an entirely new way since his death. Jackson's relationship to children is of course highly vexed. Jackson himself admitted to Martin Bashir that he slept in the same bed with children not his own and later settled out of court an accusation of child sexual abuse.[33]

In the light of these allegations, Jackson's children—who were all born after the first of two trials for child sexual abuse—were always a focus of public scrutiny and anxiety. Jackson's first two children, Michael and Paris, were born during his brief second marriage to Deborah Jeanne Rowe. He received full custody when they divorced, and she has had almost no public presence or connection to the children. His third child, Prince Michael (nicknamed "Blanket"), was conceived via artificial insemination using Jackson's sperm and an unidentified donor egg. During Jackson's lifetime, the children were hardly ever seen. The few times they were photographed, they wore masks or some other kind of covering on their faces. Jackson notoriously dangled the youngest over a balcony in Berlin (while his head was covered with a blanket), prompting Jackson to make a public apology.[34]

During his lifetime, then, the children's veiled visibility was read only in reference to their father's perverse body. Their mothers absent and unknown, the veiled children became, like the chimp Bubbles before them, innocent victims of Jackson's mental illness. That Jackson's most successful days as a musician and philanthropist were already behind him only strengthened this impression, as his eccentricity was no longer read as genius but as the result of a man whose life had been twisted by the public eye.

Jackson's identity as a father was redeemed by his death. We've already seen how Sharpton made a point of speaking to Jackson's children in his eulogy. Much as Earl Spencer's pledge to the princes solidified Diana's motherhood as her rightful legacy, Sharpton's words constructed a legacy for Jackson, a corpus in which his paternity was not tainted or perverse but misunderstood and tragic. "Wasn't nothing strange about your Daddy," Sharpton asserted. "It was strange what your daddy had to deal with. But he dealt with it, he dealt with it for us!" Publicity and visibility were the unusual forces Jackson "had to deal with" to spread his "love message."

FIGURE 13. Paris Jackson speaks for the first time in public at her father's live memorial, with the casket clearly visible in the bottom right of the image. Getty Images.

Even as televisual liveness brought the reality of the casket and its contents into our living rooms, Jackson's children suddenly became audible and visible. After Sharpton had reconstructed Jackson's paternity, for the first time ever, Paris, Michael, and Blanket appeared on-stage, unmasked. Surrounded by the Jackson family, Paris spoke through tears: "Ever since I was born Daddy was the best father you could ever imagine. I just wanted to say I love him so much."

No one had ever seen their faces before or heard their voices. In the shadow of their father's casket, the children become themselves embodied, subject to the same scrutiny: do they "look black"? Are they talented? Are they OK? The Jackson family would go on to fight over care of the children, and Paris Jackson would have a very public suicide

attempt. Joe Jackson, the children's grandfather, said in a 2013 interview that Blanket Jackson, once properly "trained up," has his father's
star quality.[35] One can only expect that the coming years will offer us
more Jacksons to consume and comment on, their bodies inexorable
referents to their father.

What lies outside of these legacies—of the British royal family and
of the King of Pop—are the illegitimate children. I mean that in the
specific sense Derrida has given the term to refer to polysemia: seeds
that missed their mark, perhaps, meaning that is otherwise than proper,
whose paternity is uncertain and contested.[36] The rumor that Diana was
pregnant with Dodi al-Fayed's child persists, though the 2007 inquest
effectively disproved it. In 2014, a report claimed to have DNA evidence
that the singer Brandon Howard was Jackson's biological son, born out
of the real-life romance portrayed in the song "Billie Jean."[37] Whether
these are true biological children is not the point: the point is that each
corpus also includes its own double, a shadow corpus, "illegitimate"
and disavowed. This illegitimate corpus reinforces the proper corpus
by making explicit the legitimacy of the recognized heirs.

The importance of the illegitimate corpus is that it is the body that is
not properly funneled into the late capitalist economy of production and
reproduction. Diana's body as a site of illicit pleasure—extramarital,
nonmaternal pleasure—is not marketable in the same way as Diana's
body, virgin breeding ground of the future King of England. Insofar
as the body of this King (like that of the King of Pop) is not a body
politic but a commodity fetish, the illegitimate corpus challenges the
fetish and lays bare the relations that create it. Brandon Howard claims
he wants no part of Jackson's fortune—which of course did not exist at the time of the singer's death, when he was $30 million in debt.
Mohamed al-Fayed's Herrods has been sold, and the shrine to Diana
and Dodi, complete with the (possibly apocryphal) engagement ring
he gave her, functions as a crass tourist trap and not a dignified (and
thus infinitely more marketable) royal tribute. The illegitimate corpus
points, therefore, to the ways in which grief is monetized through the
body, through the inheritance of a literal pound of flesh.

Conclusion

COMMUNICATING WITH THE CORPSE

> Revolution can only consist in the abolition of the
> separation from death.
> **BAUDRILLARD**, *Symbolic Exchange and Death*

The examples in this book have traced an arc wherein the corpse has retreated ever further from the visual field of mass-mediated mourning. From the embalmed corpse of the nation seeking to ensure a photographic reference, to the photograph of atrocity that erupts in the visual field like its own entity, and finally to the invisible corpse of the tabloid body that ensures its ongoing viability as commodity, each of these assemblages makes an ideologically invested statement about the corpse as material object. The corpse's progressive disappearance from the visual field is an index of its prohibition; its permeation of representational elements from embalmed flesh to photographic object and finally to invisible essence indexes the fascination with that missing piece of the real that navigates our experience of death as an imagined and individual event.

Each of these is a corpus, a body of texts and objects rigged to articulate death to a meaningful "reality" as its final signifier. None of these, however, constitutes a meaningful *encounter* with the dead as such. They do not disrupt what Deleuze calls representational thinking: an encounter shatters existing categories of thought rather than affirming them. Much like Levinas's face, the encounter (which is a more apt term when we are dealing with the dead than with living others) acknowledges alterity without assimilating it.[1]

Kittler called archival media the realm of the dead. We might instead follow Baudrillard and call it a ghetto: so-called immortality is a segregated space with no relation to the world of the living. If belief in a spiritual immortality has waned, we are more entrenched than ever in the technical immortality of archival media.[2] Archival media render immortal time fundamentally linear, moving backward and forward on the spools of the same track. They are endlessly repeatable, Bazin's "death every afternoon."[3] They are not, however, a space of encounter or exchange. Any discovery can only come from vigilant scrutiny of the text—the dream of analog media as an infinitely faithful index.[4] Discovery of what was always already there is not the same as openness to an unimagined encounter.

We must forge a vocabulary and a habit of thought that attune us to a communication with the dead. By its very nature, any encounter with the dead is radically asymmetrical, disruptive of value equivalencies and linear exchanges. To encounter death is to face that which cannot be assimilated by reason, that which cannot be reduced to an equivalent expression in a third term. Rather than a universal imaginary, death then becomes a living experience of alterity. We cannot more desperately need a critical vocabulary and revolutionary practice that brings us bodily into proximity to the fullness of difference.

If we no longer assimilate the dead to immortality, either of mediated memory or religious afterlife, but instead grant their deaths a social status, then we can begin to recuperate our own sense of loss. The dead are very much departed; we cannot see or touch them in the same ways we once did.[5] This fact is in itself sorrowful and baffling, but without the space to encounter it as real, to ritually prepare for it, we cannot then find other ways to see and touch, other kinds of commune-ication with the dead. As in the staging of the play *Our Town,* where the dead sit separately, invisible, their commentary on the living unheard, we have relegated our own sadness to mere absence and thus foreclosed any communication that does not appear as a dialogue between presences. The dead have things to teach us, and they have things to say. Their bodies hold secrets of disappearance and flux. When we banish them, we banish these things with them. We also banish our own sadness.

Now, the last thing I want to do is privilege a model of communication based on dialogue between two sovereign and self-contained presences.[6] Quite the contrary—I am asserting that the dominance of such a model forecloses necessary communication with the dead because it renders it unintelligible. I follow John Durham Peters in the conviction that communication is made of stuttering gaps and incommensurabilities.[7] I think that insight captures the pathos of communication—the ways in which our togetherness is shot through with confusion and alienation. If fusion were possible, it would be banal; that we ever feel something like connection is a testament to the radicality of communication, its heterogeneity and provisional fleetingness. This is something Levinas understood, too, when he put ethics before ontology.[8] To conceive of communication as nonlinear does not mean to abandon ethics or equality. Rather, it is to strive continuously for something that is impossible because it is the right thing to do—because the striving matters. In the striving is the meaning, and this is what we have lost.

Communication with the dead is the classic case of incommensurate dialogue. They cannot speak back to us in the same language we use to speak to them. The dead speak to us in dreams, if they speak at all; we speak to them silently or in prayer. When we light candles or visit gravestones or tend a garden or visit a favorite spot, we are seeking them in the places that are ritually marked with absence. When we buy an album or watch a movie or look at photographs, we are doing something else. Those aren't the dead but the undead. Like Freud's uncanny (and the death drive that Baudrillard works so hard, too hard, to dismantle), recordings of the dead are nauseating repetitions. We may be different when we go to them, but what they offer us is always the same. It is a denial of death that renders us melancholic because, in its cheerful facsimile of life, it is a haunting. I am not saying that the connection we have with these texts is inauthentic or secondary; I am saying that it is not the same thing as communication with the dead.

What does all this have to do with production and reproduction of social conditions? What kind of revolution are we talking about, in the end? If the dead are those with whom we no longer have congress, then we do not trade with them. We cannot extract from them any surplus labor. The image of the dead body—or the image of the body in life of someone who is now dead—becomes a kind of relic that conceals the social relations that constitute it. Michael Jackson is no longer producing surplus value, because he is dead (lucky devil!). But somebody somewhere is sitting for hours wrapping posthumous CDs in cellophane, someone somewhere is packing the boxes for shipment, someone somewhere is loading and unloading containers. These someones constitute the ever growing world of what Agamben called "bare life," those whose existence is structurally marginalized to the point where life is reduced to survival and death constitutes only a release from toil.[9] Their labor is collected under the cipher of Michael Jackson: their dead labor, congealed as capital, constitutes the corpse of Michael Jackson.

We exile and annihilate this labor just as we exile and annihilate the actual corpse. In reducing laboring bodies to bare life—to life stripped of all but survival—we also rob them of a proper and meaningful death.[10] Perhaps this is what Baudrillard meant when he called the separation of the dead primary, a condition of possibility for the rational mode of capitalist production. Those who were never alive cannot ever be dead. Labor itself continues ceaselessly, invisibly: every time a factory burns or a mine collapses, it only calls attention to the fact that these lives are not only expendable but nonexistent, brought into being only by their sudden visibility, by the exception—the ceasing of labor—that proves the rule.

Mourning is labor, too. It's no accident that we call it the "work of mourning."[11] It is a process that takes time and effort and must by definition be experienced in a direct and personal way. Mourning calls on rituals, relics, tears, and stillness. It draws on a system of meaning otherwise than the representational thinking favored by the capitalist mode of social reproduction. It is an encounter with loss where loss cannot be assimilated but must be somehow permitted. It is decomposition in all of its horrifying mystery: that someone can be unique and irreplaceable and deeply cherished, and yet also anonymously and prosaically biological. Religion divides the body from the soul in an attempt to solve this mystery, but souls are cold comfort. We can't hold them. In the best possible interpretation of religion (and this from someone who was raised by secular humanists), we know it's cold comfort, and we hold it to ourselves as a way of apprehending mystery. Death is only ever imaginary: it is the place we cannot reach. To mourn is to teach oneself to live with that place, with its disruption—not to seal it over.

Our treatment of the dead indexes our treatment of the living. Our mourning practices index our labor practices. In both cases, what we see is an extirpation of the body itself in its laboring or decomposing physicality, in its fleshy fullness and messy outlines. I am not talking about some kind of sexual liberation or celebration of pleasure. I'm talking about apprehending the flesh as such. Bare life treats the flesh as meat. We pay only as much as keeps the worker alive. When he dies, we complete the process of extirpation by moving on, filling the post, training the replacement. The slow stillness of grief has no place. One cannot lie down for six months and cry. We no longer wear mourning to indicate that, even despite outward appearances, despite appearing, we are ourselves elsewhere, somewhere underground where that beloved flesh is returning to nothing. Lincoln used to write always on mourning stationery, after his son's death. Imagine if every e-mail and text message you sent bore a black flag for years after the loss of a loved one! How simple, and how profound. It says nothing: it is an absence observed.[12]

Popular and academic discourse about media are both preoccupied with the question of bodies—whether we need them still, whether they've become obsolete with the proliferation of digital and virtual technologies, whether they are atrophied or obese or overstimulated. What seems to be harder to craft is a discourse that problematizes—in the specific sense Foucault gives the term of questioning assumptions and asking what lies outside the question as posed—the duality of the mind and the body.[13] More and more, however, feminist and feminist materialist analyses of media, as well as the growing sphere of production studies and media phenomenology, must go "beyond the body"[14] and look at the interconnectedness, indeed even the prosthetic or parasitic interdependence, of flesh and machine.

This interdependence must, crucially, be understood as asymmetrical, as nondialogic, as much a relation of mourning and loss as one of connection and extension. That is the ethics of what is at stake here. Yes, bodies and selves are leaky. They leach into one another; the self-contained, sovereign, enclosed subject or consciousness is as partial a story as the deterministic, performative body. Bodies, images, sounds, machines, texts, and inorganic objects assemble and reassemble into a corpus whose interrelations, while determinate, are not fixed. But the "leaky" metaphor fails to take into account radical difference, the kind of oil-and-water irreducibility that we must be able to apprehend if we are to listen for what the dead have to teach us and work with them to imagine a better world.

As Andrejevic cannily illustrates in the case of reality television,

FIGURE 14. "Staying alive for as long as we live" strikes me as an unusually blatant figure for bare life, particularly because this truck is delivering meals to the group home for adults living with cerebral palsy and other disabilities located on the first floor of my building in Brooklyn, New York. Photograph by the author.

the attitude of the "savvy" or cynical viewer who debunks the image's indexicality is a response to the latter's pervasiveness—that is, the popular claim of the image to provide access, truth, authenticity, and so on. Indexicality as a means by which corpses become meaningful cultural entities participates in this kind of belief in access to the real—a binary belief fraught with the contingent investments of the body's relationship to the visual or the real's relationship to the symbolic.

The savvy viewer rolls her eyes at such naive claims, citing the mechanism of fame as pervasive inauthenticity. Following Žižek, Andrejevic notes a negative materiality in which the lack around which the symbolic is organized becomes not the receding horizon of the thing-in-itself but a necessarily absent element for the symbolic's mediating role between the imaginary and the real:

> It is the mediation of symbolic efficacy that provides the imaginary with purchase on the real. The debunking of the symbolic order (which is achieved paradoxically by its expansion to the point that there remains nothing for it to mediate) sacrifices the freedom it ostensibly secures.[15]

In other words, both the naive claim to authenticity in the indexical image and the savvy response misunderstand the necessary relationship between the symbolic world as a mediator between the world as it is and the world as we might like it to be. This is not only the space where theory operates—it is also what motivates political action, for example, which is why Andrejevic suggests that the expansion of the symbolic to the point that it no longer mediates actually destroys the potential for freedom of action and leaves us with nothing but dull cynicism.

To be clear, I am not claiming that the corpse itself becomes a kind of "kernel of the real" that anchors subsequent signification. Rather, representations of a corpse become the agent for the rescue of the symbolic order, functioning to mediate between the (unknown) truth of the deceased life and the imagined future for which the legacy is constructed. Though indexicality is popularly read as a privileged relationship to the real, these cases reveal that the materiality of the corpse is found only in its ability to *differ* from the deceased—as it must. Photographs of corpses, like embalmings, disavow that difference when they are read indexically.

What, then, are the deterritorializing moments in the corpus of the nation, or of the suffering other, or of the tabloid martyr? Is the work of mourning absolutely monetized, or does it happen in ways that run counter to late capitalist value production? I don't just mean moments of contradiction but also currents that run otherwise, threads that escape the weave? And if we have tried to follow those threads here, what have we found?

We have found that the body itself is crucial to the meaningfulness of all these assemblages. Each corpus calls on us to imagine a better world, a different world, in the name of the deceased. If Sharpton's eulogy worked to reimagine Jackson's image as uncoupled from his essential blackness, then Mexican uses of Jackson in Day of the Dead imagery work outside of Sharpton's logic of appearances and essences. Michael Jackson Day of the Dead figurines—and there are many— make use of the singer's ambiguous appearance to morph him into the anonymity of a skeleton, while his sparkling glove or aviator sunglasses signify his cultural identity. It is precisely the body in its material ambiguity that furnishes the basis for these representations and allows them to function in a very real ritual of communication with the dead. Similarly, the contested body of Eva Perón becomes a site for an entirely different kind of identification in the short story "Evita vive (en cada hotel organizado)" by Néstor Perlongher. The corpse of Evita returns, not to the statehouse, but to a squat house, frolicking with men and women, black and white, transgender and queer alike—the biggest *loca* of them all. These and other configurations of the corpses constitute a communication with the dead that not only relies on Kittler's archive, the static realm of the dead, but stages a kind of encounter between incommensurate entities, each of which determines and is determined by the other.

There is a parallel between the dominance of the dialogic model of communication, which presupposes an equal exchange between two self-contained and self-aware sovereign presences, and the capitalist mode of social reproduction in which all things are expressed as monetary equivalencies. We imagine communication as exchange because exchange is the form of all of our relations under capitalism. But there are relations that are fundamentally asymmetrical that we cannot theorize so long as our media theory depends on a dialogic

FIGURE 15. A Michael Jackson Day of the Dead figurine, complete with diamond glove and aviator glasses. Photograph by the author.

model. This is part of what is implicated in a materialist study of media: the notion of a communication between or among radically distinct entities, a communication irreducible to a mediating third term. This kind of radical asymmetry characterizes our ethical relationship to others, it characterizes our relationship to divinity and to the world of animals, nature, and things—and it is the fundamental modality of our relationship to the dead. Inadequacies in the ways we conceptualize communication have very real, lived, ethical consequences in the relations of everyday life. We need to communicate with the dead in ways that are outside capitalist exchange, which happens only at the symbolic level. We have a fantasy of transcendence that reinscribes the dialogic mode of communication. Posthumous Michael Jackson albums are not a mode of communication with the dead—they are an exchange. We need to find a way to speak to the dead and, perhaps more crucially, to listen to them, so that we can know how to better live. Their deaths are not simply a canceling of debts or an isolation from the sphere of exchange but a space of radical alterity that calls to us, daily, and that we must find ears to hear.

ACKNOWLEDGMENTS

Perhaps because this is my first book, I feel as though I ought to thank every person I've ever met and acknowledge every experience as a tiny but inexorable step toward this longed-for end. Instead, I'll try to contain myself and thank the following people in reverse chronological order, with the caveat that, really, pretty much everybody and everything that ever happened until now has led toward the completion of this book.

Thanks to my colleagues and friends at Fordham University. Much of the writing for this book was done during a funded Faculty Fellowship. Generous support from the College of Arts and Sciences Ames Fund helped defray the cost of image permissions. My teaching in and conversations with the faculty of the Department of Communication and Media Studies have enriched this work in multiple ways. Eunice Kim was an excellent research assistant; Shira Grife brought me books when I was too pregnant to move. To Shira and also Cosette Carlomusto I want to say that their belief in me as a teacher made me a better one. Special thanks to my colleagues Amy Aronson, Jennifer Clark, Beth Knobel, and Alice Marwick for reading and workshopping portions of the manuscript and to Robin Andersen for her guidance in finding a publisher.

As junior faculty awash in post–grad school malaise, I found new mentors and friends who generously offered the gift of their conversation about ideas, work, and academic life. Jenny Clark was my first friend at Fordham, and I could not have finished this book without her steadfast support and encouragement. Amit Pinchevski is an invaluable interlocutor: intense, interested, and engaged with all topics theoretical, morbid, and memorious. Roopali Mukherjee took me seriously when I was struggling to articulate questions of race and the corpse. Diane

Negra was an enthusiastic editor of work on embodiment that helped me take myself seriously. The Morbid Anatomy Library, and now Museum, curated by the impeccable Joanna Ebenstein, is an ongoing site of inspiration and fellowship, and during my early days in New York it provided me with a space outside the university to pursue my ideas for a broader audience.

John Troyer started out as a citation in my dissertation and ended up as a mentor and dear friend. He gave me the great gift of his support both as reader and interlocutor. As an undertaker's son and a superhero of death studies, John can be counted on to know all the grisly details (it's a *gold* coffin, dude) and, best of all, for eager and unflinching discussion of all things morbid. That he is as a person both lovely and generous is only the icing on the (anatomical Venus) cake.

Grateful thanks to Carrie Rentschler for inviting me to speak at McGill University and for giving me the best kind of feedback: unflinching, thorough, and utterly constructive. Colleagues in that department, in particular Amelia Jones, engaged me in the kind of challenging dialogue that helped me to solidify and clarify key ideas. Carrie is a true mentor: generous in conversation, full of ideas and suggestions, she always holds me accountable to the best versions of my ideas, better versions indeed than they were before she engaged them.

Jonathan Sterne read the manuscript with attention and enthusiasm and, much like Carrie (with whom he happens to be partnered, as excellent people have a way of finding one another), seemed to find the best in what I was saying even when I didn't yet know it. Every first-time author should get a Hanukkah gift, as I did, of such a reader—so careful, respectful, and constructive. Jonathan urged me to cop to the politics of what I was trying to say; Carrie made sure I remembered exactly why that's important to do carefully and with precision. Later on, Louis-Georges Schwartz helped me think through the concept of labor in a way that moved me toward the book's more radical stakes and continues to challenge me to work toward ends that are only gestured at here. I think honestly that might have been the hardest part, and I couldn't have done it without each of them.

This book started as a dissertation at the University of Iowa on the embalmed corpse of Eva Perón. Deep gratitude to David Depew, who squinted at a confused MFA student wondering whether to pursue a PhD, jammed his last two fingers in the corner of his mouth for a minute to think, and said, "Well, it's all really about coming to grips with mortality, isn't it?" As I moved through the program at Iowa, I also had my world rocked by Mark "Doesn't Anyone Even Believe in False Consciousness Anymore?!!" Andrejevic, Daniel Balderston (who stepped in with characteristic grace), and Russell Valentino.

Michael Mario Albrecht taught me to enjoy karaoke, reminded me how awesome my husband is, and challenged me on my hipster authenticity issues. Erica Stein is my favorite Erica, and not only because she remembers everything. Jennifer Fleeger, Gina Giotta, Joe Klapper, and Kevin McDonald: here's to a houseboat in Amsterdam, or a cottage in the Berkshires, or a ranch in Big Sur, or wherever really, because anywhere we get together (our children now included) is the best kind of fun.

How can I thank John Peters? I can't: saying thank you feels like saying good-bye, and we agreed a long time ago not to do that. Instead, I offer this book as part of our ongoing conversation, shot through as it is with gaps and digressions and, most of all, with deeply felt regard.

Last, thanks to my family: Penelope and Hilary Schwartz, who always believe in me, and Rick and Sandy Schaefer, who are "in-laws" in name only. If this book isn't dedicated to Peter Schaefer, it's because I've dedicated something far more important to him, or rather, we are together dedicated: to our life, our children, the project of doing and thinking and being together in this world, which he makes better just by being in it. All that I am and do is always with you, always with love.

NOTES

INTRODUCTION

1 W. J. T. Mitchell and Mark B. N. Hansen, eds., *Critical Terms for Media Studies* (Chicago: University of Chicago Press, 2010), 50.

2 Christine Quigley, *The Corpse: A History,* new ed. (Jefferson, N.C.: McFarland, 2005).

3 André Bazin, "Death Every Afternoon," in *Rites of Realism: Essays on Corporeal Cinema,* 27–31 (Durham, N.C.: Duke University Press, 2002).

4 Gilles Deleuze and Félix Guattari, *A Thousand Plateaus: Capitalism and Schizophrenia,* trans. Brian Massumi (Minneapolis: University of Minnesota Press, 1987).

5 Julia Kristeva, "Approaching Abjection," *Oxford Literary Review* 5, no. 1–2 (1982): 125–49.

6 Ernst Kantorowicz, *The King's Two Bodies: A Study in Mediaeval Political Theology* (Princeton, N.J.: Princeton University Press, 1997).

7 André Bazin and Hugh Gray, "The Ontology of the Photographic Image," *Film Quarterly* 13, no. 4 (1960): 4–9.

8 Elaine Scarry, *The Body in Pain: The Making and Unmaking of the World* (New York: Oxford University Press, 1987).

9 Sharon Sliwinski, *Human Rights in Camera* (Chicago: University of Chicago Press, 2011).

10 Kristeva, "Approaching Abjection."

11 Lilie Chouliaraki, "The Theatricality of Humanitarianism: A Critique of Celebrity Advocacy," *Communication and Critical/Cultural Studies* 9, no. 1 (2012): 1–21.

12 An icon is a representation that has intrinsic religious power. Religious icons do not just represent the deity, they are also themselves divine, having divine power. As such, the term *icon* here is meant to invoke

structures of belief both secular and otherwise but also the paradoxical relationship between the physical and the spiritual implied by the term. Speaking of Christ, Saint Paul said, "He is the image of the invisible God"—and sparked centuries of debate over the precise relationship implied between the flesh, the image, the invisible, and the deity. An iconography of the flesh, then, is a study of the paradoxical relationship between the image and the invisible that is invoked in one of the most universal and most terrible experiences of the flesh—death.

13 Barbie Zelizer, *About to Die: How News Images Move the Public,* 1st ed. (New York: Oxford University Press, 2010).

14 The portrait is also the cover of her book *La razon de mi vida,* the bible of Peronist propaganda. It is thus one as familiar to Argentines as, say, the image of Lincoln on the five dollar bill.

15 Geoffrey Gorer, "The Pornography of Death," *Berkeley Book of Modern Writing* 3 (1956): 56–62.

16 Jean Baudrillard, *Symbolic Exchange and Death,* trans. Ian Hamilton Grant (London: Sage, 1993).

17 Antonius C. G. M. Robben, *Death, Mourning, and Burial: A Cross-Cultural Reader* (New York: John Wiley, 2009), location 263.

18 Beth A. Conklin, *Consuming Grief: Compassionate Cannibalism in an Amazonian Society* (Austin: University of Texas Press, 2001).

19 Anne M. Straus, "The Meaning of Death in Northern Cheyenne Culture," *Plains Anthropologist* 23, no. 79 (1978): 1–6.

20 Conklin, *Consuming Grief.*

21 Antonius C. G. M. Robben, "State Terror in the Netherworld: Disappearance and Reburial in Argentina," in *Death Squad: The Anthropology of State Terror,* 91–113 (Philadelphia: University of Pennsylvania Press, 2000).

22 Philippe Ariès, *The Hour of Our Death: The Classic History of Western Attitudes toward Death over the Last One Thousand Years* (New York: Vintage Books, 2008).

23 John Troyer, "Embalmed Vision," *Mortality* 12, no. 1 (2007): 22–47.

24 Bazin and Gray, "Ontology of the Photographic Image."

25 This includes a long list of commentators. Besides the Bazin essay quoted earlier, pieces that explicitly address these themes are Walter Benjamin, "Little History of Photography," in *Selected Writings,* vol. 2, ed. Michael W. Jennings, Howard Eiland, and Gary Smith, trans. Edmund Jephcott and Kingsley Shorter, 507–30 (Cambridge, Mass.: Belknap Press of Harvard University Press, 1999); Roland Barthes, *Camera Lucida,* trans. Richard Howard (New York: Hill and Wang,

1981); and Susan Sontag, *On Photography,* 1st ed. (New York: Picador, 2001). Sontag, for example, comments that all photographs are memento mori (15).

26 Jonathan Sterne, *The Audible Past: Cultural Origins of Sound Reproduction* (Durham, N.C.: Duke University Press, 2003), 292. Sterne is documenting the history of sound recording, which he places alongside embalming, canning, and other preservation techniques. *Audible Past* thus makes an excellent case for embalming as a medium, though its main objectives obviously lie elsewhere.

27 Troyer, "Embalmed Vision."

28 Jonathan Crary, *Techniques of the Observer: On Vision and Modernity in the 19th Century* (Cambridge, Mass.: MIT Press, 1992).

29 Patrice Petro, ed., *Fugitive Images: From Photography to Video* (Bloomington: Indiana University Press, 1995).

30 James J. Farrell, *Inventing the American Way of Death, 1830–1920* (Philadelphia: Temple University Press, 1980), 159.

31 Quigley, *Corpse,* 62.

32 Barbie Zelizer characterizes the "about to die" photograph as having a kind of subjunctive, "as if" function, allowing viewers to unconsciously imagine that the outcome that is not depicted (death) never happened. Modern embalming arguably performs the same function in a different mood—a future perfect that erases the trace of death and makes an image of the deceased "as if" she were sleeping. See Zelizer, *About to Die,* 12–15.

33 Gina Giotta, "Disappeared: Erasure in the Age of Mechanical Writing," PhD diss., University of Iowa, 2010. Giotta's chapter "Victorian Photoshop" collects a number of useful observations about early photography and the tension between iconic resemblance and the libidinal investments of bourgeois portraiture.

34 For more on death masks, see Margaret M. Green, trans., *Undying Faces: A Collection of Death Masks* (Breinigsville, Pa.: Kessinger, 2003), originally published by Leonard and Virginia Woolf in 1929. A theoretical link to the indexicality of the photograph is detailed in Louis Kaplan, "Photograph/Death Mask: Jean-Luc Nancy's Recasting of the Photographic Image," April 2010.

35 Jay Ruby, *Secure the Shadow: Death and Photography in America* (Cambridge, Mass.: MIT Press, 1999), 52–54.

36 Ibid.

37 For example, an 1846 advertisement for Boston firm Southworth and Hawes states, "We take great pains to have Miniatures of Deceased

Persons agreeable and satisfactory, and they are often so natural as to seem, even to Artists, in a deep sleep." Cited in Floyd Rinhart and Marion Rinhart, *The American Daguerreotype*, 1st ed. (Athens: University of Georgia Press, 1981), 299.

38 Charles E. Orr, "Post-Mortem Photography," *Philadelphia Photographer* 10 (1877): 200–201.

39 Josiah Southworth, "A Panel Discussion on Technique," *Philadelphia Photographer* 10 (1873): 279–80.

40 Ruby, *Secure the Shadow*, 16.

41 Troyer, "Embalmed Vision," 30.

42 Robert Wesley Habenstein, *The History of American Funeral Directing*, 5th ed. (Milwaukee, Wis.: National Funeral Directors Association, 2001), 212.

43 Sterne, *Audible Past*, 295; Habenstein, *History of American Funeral Directing*, 334–35.

44 The change can be compared to what happens to an egg white when it is boiled. See Christine Quigley, *Modern Mummies: The Preservation of the Human Body in the Twentieth Century* (Jefferson, N.C.: McFarland, 2006), 5; Robert Mayer, *Embalming: History, Theory, and Practice*, 5th ed. (New York: McGraw-Hill Medical, 2011), 113.

45 Troyer, "Embalmed Vision," 30. In contrast, Egyptian embalmings included removal of viscera and even the brains by hand and then preserving them in separate jars. Here the purpose was preservation as such, not preservation of the appearance of life.

46 Habenstein, *History of American Funeral Directing*, 448.

47 Jean-Nicolas Gannal, *History of Embalming, and of Preparations in Anatomy, Pathology, and Natural History*, trans. Richard Harlan (Charleston, N.C.: BiblioBazaar, 2009); Habenstein, *History of American Funeral Directing*, 328.

48 Habenstein, *History of American Funeral Directing*, 217, emphasis mine.

49 Troyer, "Embalmed Vision," 39.

50 This argument matches Carey's observations about the telegraph. See James W. Carey, "Space, Time, and Communications: A Tribute to Harold Innis," in *Communication as Culture, Revised Edition: Essays on Media and Society*, new ed. (New York: Routledge, 1992), 142–72.

51 Marshall McLuhan and Lewis H. Lapham, *Understanding Media: The Extensions of Man*, 1st ed. (Cambridge, Mass.: MIT Press, 1994), 61–65.

52 Lock excellently unpacks the economy of the gift, thus rendering the

rhetoric of "organ donation" suspect under late capitalism. See Margaret Lock, *Twice Dead: Organ Transplants and the Reinvention of Death,* 1st ed. (Berkeley: University of California Press, 2001), 316–19.

53 Jane Bennett, *Vibrant Matter: A Political Ecology of Things* (Durham, N.C.: Duke University Press, 2010); B. Brown, "Thing Theory," *Critical Inquiry* 28, no. 1 (2001): 1–22.

54 Bennett, *Vibrant Matter.*

1. THE BODY OF THE NATION

1 Bazin and Gray, "Ontology of the Photographic Image."

2 Kantorowicz, *King's Two Bodies,* xviii.

3 Lenin's body remains on view in his tomb in Red Square, Moscow, but there is periodic talk of burying the body, which (as we will see) has deteriorated over time and needs quite extensive upkeep.

4 Deleuze and Guattari, *A Thousand Plateaus.*

5 Kantorowicz, *King's Two Bodies.*

6 Carlos Fuentes, *Christopher Unborn* (Champaign, Ill.: Dalkey Archive Press, 2005), 18.

7 See, e.g., Paul Koudounaris's introduction to *The Empire of Death: A Cultural History of Ossuaries and Charnel Houses* (New York: Thames and Hudson, 2011). Koudounaris cites Baudrillard's *Symbolic Exchange and Death* as the source of his assertion that the modern attitude toward the dead is characterized by its separation from life.

8 Margrit Shildrick, *Leaky Bodies and Boundaries: Feminism, Postmodernism, and (Bio)ethics* (New York: Routledge, 1997).

9 Walter Benjamin et al., *The Origin of German Tragic Drama,* reprint ed. (New York: Verso, 2009); Theodor W. Adorno and Theodor Wiesengrund Adorno, *Negative Dialectics,* 2nd ed. (New York: Bloomsbury Academic, 1981).

10 See http://rogerjnorton.com/Lincoln51.html for a thorough account of Lincoln's funeral train's route and the details of his mourning at each stop.

11 Eyal Naveh, *Crown of Thorns: Political Martyrdom in America from Abraham Lincoln to Martin Luther King, Jr.* (New York: New York University Press, 2012).

12 Ibid., 66.

13 As Barbie Zelizer has extensively documented in her *Covering the Body,* the assassination of JFK was the first mass-mediated mourning of a dead president. Zelizer, *Covering the Body: The Kennedy Assasination,*

the Media, and the Shaping of Collective Memory (Chicago: University of Chicago Press, 1992).

14 Thomas J. Craughwell, *Stealing Lincoln's Body* (Cambridge, Mass.: Belknap Press, 2009), 181–97.

15 RFK's funeral train is a notable exception to this, as is the mourning of Ronald Reagan, which took place on two coasts over two weeks. Robert Kennedy's train and its particular meaning for African Americans has clear parallels with Lincoln's death. Reagan was a more complicated case, and his extended funerals seemed as much the televised passing of a global figure as a funeral proper. However, it is important for our purposes to realize that, in both cases, the corpse was not *viewed,* nor did it *lie in state* in the way that Lincoln's body did.

16 Naveh, *Crown of Thorns.*

17 Dorothy Kunhardt and Philip B. Kunhardt, *Twenty Days: A Narrative in Text and Pictures of the Assassination of Abraham Lincoln* (New York: Castle Books, 1993).

18 HEP, "Lincolniana: Only Known Photograph of Lincoln in His Coffin," *Journal of the Illinois State Historical Society,* Autumn 1952, 252–56.

19 Kantorowicz, *King's Two Bodies,* 14.

20 Eric L. Santner, *The Royal Remains: The People's Two Bodies and the Endgames of Sovereignty* (Chicago: University of Chicago Press, 2011).

21 Ibid., xiii–xvii.

22 That these fantasies included such perversions of population management as Dr. Schraeber's anal impregnation with a race of supermen is of course not coincidental for Santner.

23 Notice that the so-called arbitrariness of the sign, which is of central importance for Saussure, is only relevant for Peirce in one of the three types: the symbol. The other two orders of signs, indices and icons, are not at all arbitrary but connected by either resemblance or causation. This decentering of the cultural or arbitrary nature of the sign allows Peirce to distinguish more precisely between culture and causation. This in turn offers media scholars a handy vocabulary for describing the interaction of the technological and the cultural without an automatic or immediate determinism. Peirce's concept of "thirdness" or reception—that a sign depends on how it is read—also offers a theorization of that same quality of arbitrariness without ascribing it to either unscientific randomness or cultural determinism. Instead, signs interact with their readers—with culture—in a variety of ways that meaningfully involve the way they are made and the connection they have with the world.

24   Charles Hartshorn and Paul Weiss, eds., *Collected Papers of Charles Sanders Peirce*, vol. 2, *Elements of Logic* (Cambridge, Mass.: Harvard University Press, 1932), 159.

25   Ibid.

26   Daniel Morgan, "Rethinking Bazin: Ontology and Realist Aesthetics," *Critical Inquiry* 32, no. 3 (2006): 443–81.

27   Barthes, *Camera Lucida.*

28   Ibid., 4.

29   "Only a photographic lens can give us the kind of image of the object that is capable of satisfying the deep need man has to substitute for it something more than a mere approximation, a kind of decal or transfer. The photographic image is the object itself, the object freed from the conditions of time and space that govern it. No matter how fuzzy, distorted, or discolored, no matter how lacking in documentary value the image may be, it shares, by the very process of its becoming, the being of the model of which it is the representation; it *is* the model." Bazin and Gray, "Ontology of the Photographic Image," 8.

30   Morgan, "Rethinking Bazin."

31   Ludwig Wittgenstein, P. M. S. Hacker, and Joachim Schulte, *Philosophical Investigations*, 4th ed. (Chichester, U.K.: Wiley-Blackwell, 2009), part II, section iv.

32   This description from the *New York Times* during the lying in state of Lincoln's corpse illustrates, in its dramatic language that strikes a modern reader as almost pornographic, how fluent the mainstream public was with the *visage* of death: "the color is leaden, almost brown; the forehead recedes sharp and clearly marked; the eyes deep sunk and close held upon the socket; the cheek bones, always high, are unusually prominent; the cheeks hollowed and deep pitted; the unnaturally thin lips shut tight and firm as if glued together, and the small chin, covered with slight beard, seemed pointed and sharp. The body is dressed in black, the white turned-over collar and the clear white gloves making a strong contrast to the black neckcloth and the leaden-hued features." Quoted in HEP, "Lincolniana."

33   John Gray, *The Immortalization Commission: Science and the Strange Quest to Cheat Death* (London: Farrar, Straus, and Giroux, 2012).

34   Jorge Luis Borges, "El Simulacro," in *El Hacedor* (Buenos Aires: Emecé, 1960), 20–21.

35   Marysa Navarro and Nicholas Fraser, *Evita: The Real Life of Eva Perón* (New York: W. W. Norton, 1996).

36   Ibid.

37 Deleuze and Guattari, *A Thousand Plateaus.*

38 Tristán Bauer, *La tumba sin paz* [Evita: The unquiet grave], documentary film (Argentina: South Productions, 1997).

39 Víctor Hugo Ghitta, "Es hora de revisar viejas heridas," *La Nación,* March 30, 1997, Sunday edition, http://www.lanacion.com.ar/66094 -es-hora-de-revisar-viejas-heridas.

40 Julia Montesoro, "Cine argentino," *La Nación,* July 20, 2002, Saturday edition, sec. Entretenimiento, http://www.lanacion.com.ar/415124 -cine-argentino.

41 Melissa Miles, "The Burning Mirror: Photography in an Ambivalent Light," *Journal of Visual Culture* 4, no. 3 (2005): 329–49.

42 Morgan, "Rethinking Bazin," 447.

43 That the mutilations themselves could be read as indexical signs pointing toward the blows the corpse received is an interesting point that testifies to the sort of ad infinitum series inherent in the nature of the index. Peirce himself acknowledged this, and indeed, toward the end of his life, he had begun to see most signs as indexes in general (especially as the three classifications are not mutually exclusive). For more on this topic, see Douglas Greenlee, *Peirce's Concept of Sign* (The Hague: Mouton, 1973), and Mary Ann Doane, *The Emergence of Cinematic Time: Modernity, Contingency, the Archive* (Cambridge, Mass: Harvard University Press, 2002).

44 A *translation* is the movement of a *saint's* remains from one site to another. I am claiming, therefore, that by setting up Evita as a saint and then narratively exhuming her to refigure the site of burial, *The Unquiet Grave* constitutes a kind of figurative translation.

45 Louis Althusser, "Ideology and Ideological State Apparatuses (Notes towards an Investigation)," in *Media and Cultural Studies: Keyworks,* 1st ed., ed. Meenakshi Gigi Durham and Douglas M. Kellner, 79–87 (New York: Wiley-Blackwell, 2005).

46 Deleuze and Guattari, *A Thousand Plateaus.*

2. MARTYRED BODIES

1 Clenora Hudson-Weems, *Emmett Till: The Sacrificial Lamb of the Civil Rights Movement* (Bloomington, Ind.: AuthorHouse, 2006).

2 The term *sacrificial lamb* obviously carries Judeo-Christian connotations that may seem out of place for Hamza al-Khateeb, who was Muslim. The tradition of martyrdom in Islam differs significantly from the Christian tradition, and I do not wish to paper over that difference.

However, this chapter is concerned with the reception of al-Khateeb's death in a Western and thus dominantly Judeo-Christian cultural context. The video I analyze is subtitled in English and intended to raise awareness among Western viewers of the plight of the Syrian people. In this sense, the martyrdom of his body is read in a Western context, even as al-Khateeb was also portrayed as a martyr locally. It's just that what *martyr* means in each of these contexts is different, and I want to make it clear that my analysis focuses on the Western reception of the video.

3 Michel Foucault, "The Right of Death and Power over Life," in *The Foucault Reader,* ed. Paul Rabinow, 258–72 (New York: Pantheon, 1984).

4 Susan Sontag, *Regarding the Pain of Others,* reprint ed. (New York: Picador, 2004).

5 Sliwinski, *Human Rights in Camera,* 5.

6 Ibid.

7 I mean *encounter* in the sense that Deleuze gives the term, as an eruption that cannot be contained or assimilated. See Gilles Deleuze and Paul Patton, *Difference and Repetition* (New York: Columbia University Press, 1995), 22.

8 There is some difference of opinion as to whether Till's death should be referred to as a "murder" or a "lynching." Though not the classic mob scene leaving "strange fruit" hanging from a tree for all to see, his death is in many senses a lynching: the vigilante killing of a black man who is seen as having outstepped the bounds of white supremacist social roles, particularly where relations with women are concerned. However, Till's death was not a spectacle the way that lynchings in the post-Reconstruction South were: the killers weighted down his body in the hopes it would not be found rather than publicly lynching him as an "example" to the rest of the community. For this reason, some writers choose to call it a murder. Because my analysis concerns the deployment of the images as political relics of a martyr to the cause of civil rights, I am using the term *lynching,* for it is the visual spectacle of his death *as reappropriated by the black community* that is of interest here. That kind of reappropriation has a history that would have been clear to African Americans in 1955, who would have remembered or grown up hearing about the NAACP's 1920s antilynching campaigns that made use of lynching photography to highlight the barbarity of lynching and taking photographs as souvenirs.

9 Jacqueline Goldsby, "The High and Low Tech of It: The Meaning of

Lynching and the Death of Emmett Till," *The Yale Journal of Criticism* 9, no. 2 (1996): 249.

10 Juan Williams, *Eyes on the Prize: America's Civil Rights Years, 1954–1965* (New York: Penguin Books, 1988), 42.

11 Hudson-Weems, *Emmett Till.*

12 Christine Harold and Kevin Michael DeLuca, "Behold the Corpse: Violent Images and the Case of Emmett Till," *Rhetoric and Public Affairs* 8, no. 2 (2005): 269.

13 The work of Ida B. Wells is a seminal examination of the intersection of racial and sexual violence in lynching. For an analysis of Wells's work and its contribution to the antilynching movement, see Hazel V. Carby, "'On the Threshold of Woman's Era': Lynching, Empire, and Sexuality in Black Feminist Theory," *Critical Inquiry* 12, no. 1 (1985): 262–77.

14 James Allen, *Without Sanctuary: Lynching Photography in America,* 1st ed., ed. James Allen (Palm Springs, Calif.: Twin Palms, 2000).

15 Harold and DeLuca, "Behold the Corpse," 270. They also state that this information was part of the documentary *Eyes on the Prize.*

16 William Bradford Huie, "The Shocking Story of Killing Approved in Mississippi," *Look,* January 24, 1956.

17 Hudson-Weems, *Emmett Till,* 14–17.

18 Mamie Till-Mobley and Christopher Benson, *Death of Innocence: The Story of the Hate Crime That Changed America* (New York: Random House, 2003).

19 Ibid., 135–36.

20 Williams, *Eyes on the Prize,* 44.

21 Hudson-Weems, *Emmett Till,* xli–xliii.

22 Williams, *Eyes on the Prize,* 57.

23 Sliwinski, *Human Rights in Camera.*

24 I refer, of course, to the watchword of the Argentine human rights trials, where *nunca más* signified not only a moral condemnation but a vision of a nation rededicated to human rights and reparations.

25 Scarry, *The Body in Pain.*

26 Harold and DeLuca, "Behold the Corpse."

27 "Something in the world forces us to think. This something is an object not of recognition but of a fundamental *encounter.*" Deleuze and Patton, *Difference and Repetition,* 139.

28 Liz Sly, "Apparent Torture of Boy Reinvigorates Syria's Protest Movement," *Washington Post,* May 29, 2011, http://www.washingtonpost.com/world/middle-east/torture-of-boy-reinvigorates-syrias-protest-movement/2011/05/29/AGPwIREH_story_1.html.

29 Liam Stack, "Hamza Ali Al-Khateeb Becomes a Symbol of Syr-
      ian Brutality," *New York Times,* May 30, 2011, http://www.nytimes
      .com/2011/05/31/world/middleeast/31syria.html.
30 Hugh Macleod and Annasofie Flamand, "Tortured and Killed: Hamza Al-
      Khateeb, Age 13—Features—Al Jazeera English," May 31, 2011, http://
      www.aljazeera.com/indepth/features/2011/05/201153185927813389
      .html.
31 Harriet Alexander, "How a 13-Year-Old Boy Became the Face of the
      Syrian Uprising," *Telegraph,* June 5, 2011, http://www.telegraph.co.uk
      /news/worldnews/middleeast/syria/8556619/How-a-13-year-old-boy
      -became-the-face-of-the-Syrian-uprising.html.
32 *Martyr—Hamza Al-Khatib the Child 13 Years Old,* 2011, http://www
      .youtube.com/watch?v=p_syR-jrWVg&feature=youtube_gdata_player.
33 Macleod and Flamand, "Tortured and Killed."
34 Ibid.
35 Alexander, "How a 13-Year-Old Boy Became the Face of the Syrian
      Uprising."
36 Liz Hazelton, "Hamza Ali Al-Khateeb the Child Martyr Tortured to
      Death by Syria's Sadistic Regime," *Mail Online,* June 1, 2011, http://
      www.dailymail.co.uk/news/article-1392684/Hamza-Ali-al-Khateeb
      -child-martyr-tortured-death-Syrias-sadistic-regime.html.
37 Alexander, "How a 13-Year-Old Boy Became the Face of the Syrian
      Uprising."
38 Macleod and Flamand, "Tortured and Killed."
39 Alexander, "How a 13-Year-Old Boy Became the Face of the Syrian
      Uprising."
40 "Hamza Al-Khatib, Syria Boy, Brutally Killed in Custody," *Huffing-
      ton Post,* May 31, 2011, http://www.huffingtonpost.com/2011/05/31
      /hamza-al-khatib-syria-boy-killed_n_869314.html.
41 Stack, "Hamza Ali Al-Khateeb Becomes a Symbol of Syrian Brutality."
42 Kelly Pearsall, *Anderson Cooper 360,* CNN, May 31, 2011.
43 Elizabeth Alexander, *Black Male: Representations of Masculinity in
      Contemporary American Art* (New York: Whitney Museum of Ameri-
      can Art, 1994), 105.
44 "Nation Horrified by Murder of Kidnaped Chicago Youth," *Jet,* Sep-
      tember 15, 1955.
45 Till-Mobley and Benson, *Death of Innocence,* unpaginated with image
      of corpse.
46 Ibid., 140.
47 Harold and DeLuca, "Behold the Corpse," 274.
48 Ibid., 277–78.

49 Ibid., 280.

50 Julia Kristeva, *Powers of Horror: An Essay on Abjection,* trans. Leon S. Roudiez (New York: Columbia University Press, 1982).

51 *Martyr—Hamza Al-Khatib the Child 13 Years Old.* I want to make a few comments about the production of this text. First, the transcript provided here is obviously a translation of the Arabic original. I do not speak Arabic and thus had to rely on the subtitles to understand the off-camera narration. Insofar as my interest is in the legibility of this corpse to a Western, primarily American audience, I take this reliance on translation to be typical of the nonlocal reception of the video. However, it must be clear that I don't know who authored the subtitles. The invisibility of translation extends to YouTube videos, so there has been no attempt to document it here; it may have been the user, abuhamad77. Many of his or her comments appear also in Arabic. Abuhamad77 is not the only user to have uploaded the video, however. The initial Al Jazeera article about al-Khateeb provides a link to the video on YouTube, which currently reads that the video is no longer available because the user who uploaded it is no longer active. The video uploaded by abuhamad77 is also not the only version on YouTube; at least one other, without subtitles, is available, as are snippets aired on *Anderson Cooper 360,* and so on. All of this makes the video truly a "viral" text in that it has multiplied and circulated in similar but nonidentical forms very rapidly, and no particular author is associated with it. These considerations inform my reading of the video and, indeed, have various repercussions for the textuality of such media forms in general and how we consider them. My intention here, however, is merely to highlight some of the issues in reading this text so as to clear the way for arguments about how this corpse becomes a legible signifier to Western, English-speaking audiences who are physically and culturally distant from the Syrian conflict.

52 Indeed, some of the English YouTube comments object to the video because it is so graphic: "I thought violence is not allowed on youtube? this is sick" (huyenngale).

53 This blurring is sometimes, depending on the version, accompanied by the subtitle "YouTube does not show explicit content," a statement that takes on macabre comicalness in the context of all that has led up to it.

54 Hazelton, "Hamza Ali Al-Khateeb the Child Martyr Tortured to Death by Syria's Sadistic Regime."

55 Zelizer, *About to Die,* 8–11.

56 Ibid., 12–15.

57 On July 26, 2012, the following post appeared above the school photograph of Hamza al-Khateeb: "Urgent . . . please respond. We received a message of warning from Face book, they consider some of the pictures we publish against their laws. Although FB is the only window that we can deliver a small part of the Syrians daily suffering and the ongoing massacres, they are warning us from publishing pictures of martyred children, and from publishing parts of massacres, and considers it against the laws of publishing!!! We were informed that if we continue to publish such scenes, this will subject the administrators account to deletion and to closing the page. We kindly ask your support for what we publish by (like and sharing what we publish). Share widely to allow this page to be the voice of Syrian children, and to be the voice of all the Syrian martyrs—In God's willing—to reach all the world . . . please respond to our call." Not only is this an interesting twist on the notion of Facebook activism—that to "Like" and share the photographs would allow the site to continue posting them—but it also asserts that Facebook is the only means to share such images, hence the urgency of the message. Now posts appear with warnings that images are graphic; one on August 6, 2012, said it had been cropped "so Facebook won't ban us." Nevertheless, the site continues, and many images are still quite graphic. They also posted a poll on July 30 asking whether the Facebook page was readers' "main source for the Syrian revolution news." Options were "Yes, it is my main source," "No" (with a request for a comment on what is), and "It is one of the main sources." According to the posted results, the majority of Facebook users do claim the page as their main source. Of course, I'm not sure what that says about anything, except that Facebook users get their news from Facebook—but it was clearly an attempt to prove to the site's administrators that their images were not just gratuitously violent but had an ethical and journalistic imperative that would legitimate them.

58 Sontag, *On Photography.*

59 Sliwinski, *Human Rights in Camera.*

60 Ibid.

3. TABLOID BODIES

1   Tina Brown, *The Diana Chronicles* (New York: Broadway Books, 2008), 444.

2 "Although ordinarily everything that the jury hears and sees will go almost immediately on the inquest website, these photographs will not go on the website for the reason that it is possible for photographs that have been pixelated to be unpixelated if they get into certain hands." Fred Attewill, "Jurors View Photos of Dying Diana," *The Guardian,* October 11, 2007, http://www.guardian.co.uk/uk/2007/oct/11/monarchy.

3 "Autopsy Reveals Michael Jackson's Secrets," CNN, http://www.cnn.com/2013/05/07/showbiz/jackson-death-trial/index.html.

4 I don't mean to imply that these images are completely unavailable or nonexistent. Images of both corpses can be found simply by searching Google images—and the one of Jackson's corpse, anyway, has the authenticating detail of the courtroom label on it. However, there is a world of difference between doing a Google search that includes these kinds of morbid "horror" images and one that includes the iconic images of their lives and even of their deaths, which do not include these images.

5 For more on the concept of "liveness" and specifically its discursive construction, see Philip Auslander, *Liveness: Performance in a Mediatized Culture* (New York: Routledge, 2008).

6 My thanks to Shannon Taggert for furnishing this stunningly apt description of Jackson's costume aesthetic during her talk at the Morbid Anatomy Museum, "Michael Jackson Betwixt/Between," on August 29, 2014.

7 Adrian Kear and Deborah Lynn Steinberg, eds., *Mourning Diana: Nation, Culture, and the Performance of Grief,* 1st ed. (New York: Routledge, 1999), 3–4.

8 "Princess Diana Graces Vanity Fair Cover amid Royal Baby Craze—See the Pic!," E! Online, http://www.eonline.com/news/443931/princess-diana-graces-vanity-fair-cover-amid-royal-baby-craze-see-the-pic.

9 "Princess Diana Digitally Altered to Look Age 50 for Newsweek; Di Would Use Facebook, Botox," *New York Daily News,* http://www.nydailynews.com/life-style/princess-diana-digitally-altered-age-50-newsweek-di-facebook-botox-article-1.132041.

10 Marc Schneider, "Michael Jackson Hologram Rocks Billboard Music Awards," Billboard, http://www.billboard.com/articles/events/bbma-2014/6092040/michael-jackson-hologram-billboard-music-awards.

11 Daniel Dayan and Elihu Katz, *Media Events: The Live Broadcasting of History* (Cambridge, Mass.: Harvard University Press, 1994).

12 Paul Frosh and Amit Pinchevski, eds., *Media Witnessing: Testimony in the Age of Mass Communication* (New York: Palgrave Macmillan, 2009).

13 Like Diana, Jackson also often visited sick children in the hospital and even paid for chemotherapy treatments and invited survivors he had helped to visit him at home. One of these children, Gavin Arvizo, would later be the accuser in the 2005 trial for child molestation. This is doubtless the reason why Jackson's humanitarian work with children is not a lasting part of his legacy.

14 Diana Spencer was born in 1961, Michael Jackson in 1958.

15 Paul Frosh, "Telling Presences: Witnessing, Mass Media, and the Imagined Lives of Strangers," in *Media Witnessing,* 59.

16 Andrew Morton, *Diana: 1961–1997 Her True Story,* rev. ed. (New York: Simon and Schuster, 1997), 278.

17 Brown, *Diana Chronicles,* 442–43.

18 "Brother's Eulogy for Diana: 'The Very Essence of Compassion,'" *New York Times,* September 7, 1997, http://www.nytimes.com/1997/09/07/world/brother-s-eulogy-for-diana-the-very-essence-of-compassion.html.

19 Ibid.

20 Kear and Steinberg, *Mourning Diana,* 15.

21 Nikki Sullivan, "'It's as Plain as the Nose on His Face': Michael Jackson, Modificatory Practices, and the Question of Ethics," *SCAN: Journal of Media, Culture, Arts* 3, no. 1 (2004), http://www.scan.net.au/scan/journal/display.php?journal_id=44.

22 In a fascinating twist to which I can't do justice here, Shannon Taggart argues that Jackson planted many of the tabloid stories about himself, most notably that he slept in an oxygen chamber and that he had purchased the bones of the so-called Elephant Man.

23 Sullivan, "It's as Plain as the Nose on His Face."

24 This quotation and others from the memorial service are my own transcription.

25 Sullivan, "It's as Plain as the Nose on His Face."

26 Jackson's lightening of his skin tone had become such a topic of ridicule by the time of his death that it was a running gag. For example, in the 2004 comedy *Hot Tub Time Machine,* the protagonists ascertain that they have indeed traveled back in time by stopping someone and asking, "What color is Michael Jackson?" When the person looks confused and answers "black" as if that were obvious, the time travelers clutch their temples and howl, realizing they have indeed been transported back to the 1980s—that mythical time before Jackson's racial identity was ambiguous.

27 There is a consistent misremembering that Jackson's "Billie Jean" was actually the first video by a black artist on MTV, which is not the case.

Interestingly enough, to search for this information online returns with language very similar to that used by Sharpton in the eulogy: that "Billie Jean" was not the first video but that it "broke barriers" by being the first *popular* video by a black artist, the first in heavy rotation. Realizing that to "break barriers" is hardly original rhetoric, it's hard to make a firm causal relationship between Sharpton's eulogy and the ways in which Jackson is remembered and memorialized online; however, the coincidence of the language is enough to establish that Jackson's contribution is remembered in terms of something like "integration" or the breaking of racial barriers. Sharpton's eulogy, like Earl Spencer's, set the tone for the work of memorialization carried on in pop culture.

28 Kear and Steinberg, *Mourning Diana, 26.*

29 The most startling proof of this change is perhaps not the studied "normalcy" of Kate and Wills but the Queen's dramatic "entrance" to the 2012 Summer Olympics in London, when she and the current 007, Daniel Craig, parachuted into the Opening Ceremony. Part *Jackass* and part meme, this kind of "stunt Queen" behavior was unthinkable in 1997.

30 "Brother's Eulogy for Diana."

31 As an indicator of just how entrenched this narrative is, a collector's edition *Vanity Fair* book about the royals includes a side-by-side comparison of Charles and Diana's courtship and marriage with William and Katherine's. The graphic is obviously intended to highlight how far we've come and how "down to earth" this new generation is, while also highlighting its glamour. Charles proposed at Buckingham Palace; William proposed in a tent on the Kenyan plain. One is certainly more "casual" and modern than the other, but neither is particularly "normal" from the standpoint of the average North American consumer of *Vanity Fair.*

32 For more on Katherine and William's royal coupledom, see my contribution, "Diana's Rings: Fetishizing the Royal Couple," to *First Comes Love: Power Couples, Celebrity Kinship, and Cultural Politics,* edited by Shelley Cobb and Neil Ewen, 155–68 (New York: Bloomsbury Academic, 2015).

33 That part of that trial depended on a long and detailed description of Jackson's penis is itself a stunning indicator of the highly charged nature of Jackson's body, not only sexually but in terms of racial identity. The trial hinged on a comparison of the boy's description of Jackson's penis (presumably from memory) with an actual photograph of it. In the course of this almost ludicrous proceeding, the pigmentation of the penis—black or white?!—was a key detail.

34 The image of Jackson dangling the child is so notorious that walking tours of Berlin include a visit to the hotel and identify the exact balcony. At one time you could also purchase a plastic model of the scene from a company specializing in three-dimensional models of notorious paparazzi photos (I own one of Britney Spears's infamous upskirt photos).

35 "Blanket Speaks Out for the First Time since His Father Michael Jackson's Death and Tells How Growing Up on Neverland Ranch Was Like 'Living at a Zoo,'" *Daily Mail,* http://www.dailymail.co.uk/news /article-2524671/Michael-Jacksons-son-Blanket-speaks-time-fathers -death.html.

36 Jacques Derrida, "White Mythology: Metaphor in the Text of Philosophy," in *Margins of Philosophy,* trans. Alan Bass, 207–71 (Chicago: University of Chicago Press, 1985).

37 "Michael Jackson's Real-Life 'Billie Jean' May Have Given Him a Son," *Vibe,* http://www.vibe.com/article/michael-jacksons-alleged-son-real -life-billie-jean.

CONCLUSION

1 Gilles Deleuze and Félix Guattari, *A Thousand Plateaus: Capitalism and Schizophrenia,* trans. Brian Massumi (Minneapolis: University of Minnesota Press, 1987).

2 Every time I plug my phone into my computer to sync it, a box pops up with the somewhat threatening message, "keep your memories safe." It's asking me whether I want to upload photos from my phone into the cloud.

3 André Bazin, "Death Every Afternoon," in *Rites of Realism: Essays on Corporeal Cinema,* 27–31 (Durham, N.C.: Duke University Press, 2002).

4 Eric W. Rothenbuhler and John Durham Peters, "Defining Phonography: An Experiment in Theory," *Musical Quarterly* 81, no. 2 (1997): 245.

5 As is so often the case, children's behavior offers remarkable insight into socialization that adults have long since internalized. Unabashed narcissists, for them death is always about their own disappearance. My daughter was about four when she started asking why I didn't have a dad. Given that I'm in the business I'm in, I didn't mince words—I explained as simply as possible that he had died a long time before she was born. Now whenever she is searching for a reason to be sad— whenever she has a feeling she can't name or explain and wants an

emotional outlet—she starts talking about Harold. Not because she misses him but because she knows that this is an acceptable outlet for sadness, a place where the adults around her agree that otherwise unseemly emotions are allowed. Flailing, as all parents must, to soothe a child even when we know it's futile, I once mumbled vague platitudes about how he is "still in our hearts." "BUT I CAN'T HUG HIM EVER IN MY WHOLE LIFE!" she wailed. Touch is what we lose when someone dies; all reciprocity is foreclosed. If the dead only speak to us in the words we give them, this renders us mute and annihilated as well.

6 This is, of course, the dominant model in much of our academic and popular thinking about communication as it has gained ascendency as the primary paradigm through which we understand our times and relations. See John Durham Peters, *Speaking into the Air: A History of the Idea of Communication* (Chicago: University of Chicago Press, 2001).

7 John Durham Peters, "The Gaps of Which Communication Is Made 1," *Critical Studies in Mass Communication* 11, no. 2 (1994): 117–40.

8 Dennis King Keenan, *Death and Responsibility: The "Work" of Levinas* (Albany: State University of New York Press, 1999); Amit Pinchevski, *By Way of Interruption: Levinas and the Ethics of Communication* (Pittsburgh, Pa.: Duquesne University Press, 2005).

9 Giorgio Agamben, *Homo Sacer: Sovereign Power and Bare Life,* 1st ed., trans. Daniel Heller-Roazen (Stanford, Calif.: Stanford University Press, 1998).

10 Ibid.

11 Pierre Fedida, "The Relic and the Work of Mourning," *Journal of Visual Culture* 2, no. 1 (2003): 62.

12 It may sound banal, but this observation is at the core of a running joke in Joel and Ethan Coen's film *The Big Lebowski.* A gang of thugs identify themselves as nihilists, clarifying, "We believe in nothing." The joke, of course, is that rather than not believing in anything, the nihilists actually put their belief in nothing itself.

13 Michel Foucault, "Polemics, Politics, and Problematizations: An Interview with Michel Foucault," interview by P. Rabinow, 1984.

14 Elizabeth Hallam, Jenny Hockey, and Glennys Howarth, *Beyond the Body: Death and Social Identity* (New York: Routledge, 1999).

15 Mark Andrejevic, *Reality TV: The Work of Being Watched* (Lanham, Md.: Rowman and Littlefield, 2003), 207.

INDEX

Adorno, Theodor, 29
Agamben, Giorgio, 105–6
Agha-Soltan, Neda, 76
Alexander, Elizabeth, 65
Al Jazeera (television network), 63, 64
Althusser, Louis, 49
Anderson Cooper 360, 64, 128n51
Andrejevic, Mark, 107–9
antilynching campaigns, 58–59, 125n8
Ara, Pedro, 41
Arab Spring (2010), 64, 75
Aramburu, Pedro, 41
archival media, 1, 3, 12, 81, 85, 87, 103–4, 110
Ariès, Philippe, 15
Assad, Bashar al-, 64, 68, 69–70, 74
assemblage: in archival media, 85–86; corpse materiality and, 4, 103; as corpus, 16, 18, 24, 50, 86, 110; difference/polysemy and, 24–25; nomadism and, 50; use of term, 4
atrocity, images of, 80–81

bare life, 105–6, 107, 108
Barthes, Roland, 37
Bashir, Martin, 100

Baudrillard, Jean, 103, 105
Bauer, Tristán, 44. *See also Unquiet Grave, The* (documentary)
Bazin, André, 3, 16, 29, 37, 38, 104
Benjamin, Walter, 29
"Billie Jean" (Jackson video), 95–96, 102, 131–32n27
Bismillah invocation, 72
bodies. *See* corpse(s); martyred bodies; tabloid bodies
body politic, 27–28, 34–36, 39
Bonasso, Miguel, 44, 45. *See also Unquiet Grave, The* (documentary)
Borges, Jorge Luis, 40
Bradley, Mamie Till, 56, 57–60, 65–66
Brown, Bill, 1
Brown v. Board of Education, 56
Bryant, Roy, 57

Cabanillas, Héctor, 45
Camilla, Duchess of Cornwall, 99
"Candle in the Wind" (Elton John song), 92
Charles, Prince of Wales, 97–99
Chávez, Hugo: display of embalmed body, 28

Chicago Defender (newspaper), 58, 59
civil rights movement, 55–61
Civil War, U.S. (1861–1865), 35
Cleveland Call and Post (newspaper), 58
Clinton, Hillary, 64
communication with the dead, 104–5, 110–12
Cooper, Anderson, 64
corpse(s): commodification of, 13, 17, 83, 86, 88; communication with, 104–5, 110–12; as corpus, 49–51; decomposition of, 4, 5, 14, 18, 20–21, 39, 67, 88, 106–7; defined, 3–4; difference/polysemy and, 24–25, 39; display of, 7, 12, 27; human finality of, 2; indexicality and, 8, 9, 12–14, 24, 49, 109; labor and, 105–6; legacy and, 5, 8, 9, 12–14, 24, 109; liminality of, 5, 7, 17, 67–68; materiality of, 1, 3, 5, 9, 24, 54, 87, 93–94, 109; mediation of, 2, 17, 23–25; progressive disappearance of, 103; realm of the dead, 1, 3, 81, 87, 103, 110; as remains, 4–5. *See also* embalming; iconic corpses; martyred bodies
corpus: in assemblage, 16, 18, 24, 50, 86, 110; corpse as, 49–51; legacy and, 16; nation, 27–28
countenance, use of term, 23
Crary, Jonathan, 17–18
Crisis (NAACP publication), 58
cultural values, 2

dead bodies. *See* corpse(s)
death: as long sleep, 23; masks, 18–19; models, 14

decomposition, 4, 5, 14, 18, 20–21, 39, 67, 88, 106–7
Deleuze, Gilles, 4, 16, 24, 44, 49–50, 61, 103
DeLuca, Kevin Michael, 67
Derrida, Jacques, 98
determinism, 2–3, 107, 122n23
Diana, Princess of Wales: bulimia, 85, 92, 99; casket, prominence of, 84, 91; children of, 97–100; corpse, absence of, 84; as iconic corpse, 6; legacy of, 85, 92, 97–102; media images of, 3; revocation of royal title, 89; Spencer eulogy for, 88–92; tabloid martyrdom of, 10–12, 85–86, 97, 102; unpublished photographs of accident, 83–84; witnessing modality of, 87
Duarte, Erminda, 45
Duarte tomb, 42–44

Elizabeth, Queen of Great Britain, 98–99, 132n29
embalming, 4–5; aesthetics of, 16, 18, 20; as corpse time, 23, 44; decay and, 39; display of iconic corpses, 7, 12, 27–29, 51; as erasure of death, 119n32; indexicality and, 8–9, 27, 29, 103, 109; mechanics of, 17, 21–22; modern technologies, 20–21, 30; photography and, 14–24, 27, 37, 51; postmortem condition and, 15–16; regulation of, 17. *See also* Jackson, Michael; Lenin, Vladimir; Lincoln, Abraham; Perón, Eva
"Evita vive (en cada hotel organizado)" (Perlongher), 110

Fayed, Dodi al-, 102
Fayed, Mohamed al-, 102
feminism, 107
Foucault, Michel, 34, 107
Freud, Sigmund, 34, 105
Frosh, Paul, 85–86
Fuentes, Carlos, 28

Gannal, Jean-Nicolas, 20, 22
"Goodbye England's Rose" (Elton
    John song), 92
Guattari, Félix, 4, 16, 24, 44,
    49–50
Gunning, Tom, 18

Habenstein, Robert, 21
Harold, Christine, 67
Harrods (department store), 102
Harry, Prince of Wales, 97–98
Harry, Prince of Wales KCVO,
    97–98
Heal the World Foundation, 86
hierarchical thinking, 49–50
Ho Chi Minh: display of
    embalmed body, 28
Hour of Our Death, The (Ariès),
    15
Howard, Brandon, 102
Hudson-Weems, Clenora, 57, 59,
    61
Huffington Post (online news
    content), 63–64
human rights, aesthetic of, 55

icon, use of term, 117–18n12
iconic corpses: commodification
    of, 13; display of, 7, 12, 27–29,
    51; politicality of, 24, 27;
    themes related to, 12; use of
    term, 6. See also Diana, Princess
    of Wales; Jackson, Michael;

Khateeb, Hamza al-; Lenin,
    Vladimir; Lincoln, Abraham;
    Perón, Eva, Till, Emmett
indexicality: corpse and, 8, 9,
    12–14, 24, 49, 109; death
    masks and, 19; in embalming/
    photography, 8–9, 27, 29, 44,
    46–47, 66, 67, 93–94, 103, 109;
    as ideology, 47–49; of martyred
    bodies, 54, 56; reality and, 109;
    vulnerability and, 9
International Criminal Court, 74

Jackson, Joe, 102
Jackson, Michael: blackness of,
    11, 80, 93, 131n26; casket,
    prominence of, 84, 87; children
    of, 99–102; corpse, absence
    of, 84, 87; Day of the Dead
    figurines, 110, 111; as iconic
    corpse, 6; labor and, 105–6;
    legacy of, 85, 94–95, 97–102,
    110, 131n13; plastic surgeries,
    85, 92–93; stigmata, 93–96;
    tabloid martyrdom of, 10–11,
    85–86, 93–97, 102; unpublished
    photographs of corpse, 83–84;
    witnessing modality of, 87
Jackson, Michael, Jr., 100–101
Jackson, Paris, 100–102
Jackson, Prince Michael (Blanket),
    100–102
Jackson Five, 95
Jet (magazine), 58, 65, 78
Jim Crow South, 57
John, Elton, 92

Kant, Immanuel, 55
Kantorowicz, Ernst, 7, 34
Katherine, Duchess of Cambridge,
    87–88, 99

Kear, Adrien, 85, 97
Kennedy, John F., 22, 121n13
Kennedy, Robert F., 122n15
Khateeb, Hamza al-: Facebook
    page on, 10, 63, 75–78, 129n57;
    as martyred corpse, 5–6, 10,
    51, 53–54, 61–65, 68, 80–81;
    torture of, 10, 61–62, 70, 73–74,
    79; video of corpse, 53, 61,
    62–64, 68–75, 79
Kim Il-sung: display of embalmed
    body, 28
Kim Jong-il: display of embalmed
    body, 28
king's two bodies, use of term, 7,
    28, 34
Kirchner, Cristina, 12
Kittler, Friedrich, 1, 3, 87, 103,
    110
Kristeva, Julia, 67–68

labor: dead, 105–6; mourning
    practices, 106–7, 110
labor unions, 60
Lamers, William, 21
leaky metaphor, 107
legacy: of civil rights movement,
    61; as commodity fetish, 85–86;
    construction of, 14; corpse
    and, 5, 8, 9, 12–14, 24, 109;
    corpus and, 16; narration of,
    2; photography and, 15–16;
    politics of, 12
Lenin, Vladimir: as iconic corpse,
    7, 29, 38–40, 44
Levinas, Emmanuel, 104, 105
Lincoln, Abraham: body of nation
    and, 30; display of corpse, 29;
    exhumed, 31; as iconic corpse,
    7, 34, 38–39; photography of
    corpse, 31–34

Lincoln, Mary Todd, 37
Lock, Margaret, 23, 120–21n52
lynching, 57, 65, 125n8. See also
    Till, Emmett

"Man in the Mirror" (Jackson
    video), 86
Mao Zedong: display of
    embalmed body, 28
Marcos, Ferdinand: display of
    embalmed body, 28
Martínez de Perón, Isabel, 6
martyred bodies, 5–6, 53–56. See
    also Khateeb, Hamza al-; Till,
    Emmet
Martyr Hamza alKatib The Child
    13 Years Old (Youtube video),
    68, 128n51. See also Khateeb,
    Hamza al-
materialism: of corpses, 1, 3,
    5, 9, 24, 54, 87, 93–94, 109;
    media and, 1–2, 24–25, 83, 107,
    110–11; use of term, 3–4
media: materialist analysis of,
    24–25, 83, 107, 110–11; space/
    time and, 23; studies, 3. See also
    archival media
mediation of corpse, 2, 17, 23–25
Michael Jackson: The Face
    (documentary), 93
Mi hermana Evita (Duarte), 45
Milem, R. J., 57
Montgomery bus boycott, 59
Morgan, Daniel, 36
mortuary rituals, 13–16. See also
    embalming; photography
mourning practices, 3, 23; as labor,
    106–7, 110; mediated, 6, 34,
    53, 103, 121n13; national, 35;
    political causes and, 6–7, 81; of
    tabloid bodies, 83, 92; visual in,

13, 18–19, 30–31, 35; Western, 13, 54
MTV, 95–96
Murray, Conrad, 84

National Association for the Advancement of Colored People (NAACP), 58–59
nation as body metaphor, 6–7, 30
necrophilia, 8
New Amsterdam News (newspaper), 58
Newsweek (magazine), 85
nomadic thinking, 49–50, 67
Nunca mas! (slogan), 80

Obama, Barack, 96

Parks, Rosa, 59
Paul, Saint, 118n12
Peirce, Charles Sanders, 36, 122n23, 124n43
Perlongher, Néstor, 110
Perón, Eva (Evita): in Duarte tomb, 42–44; as iconic corpse, 6, 7–8, 12, 29, 40–44, 49; legacy of, 8, 42, 45, 47–49; mutilation of corpse, 8, 41, 44–45, 47, 48; photographs of corpse, 41, 45–48; recovery of corpse, 7–8, 41; short story about corpse of, 110. *See also Unquiet Grave, The* (documentary)
Perón, Juan, 42
photography: "about to die," 76, 77, 119n32; aesthetics of death and, 15–16; embalming and, 14–24, 27, 37, 51; funeral portraits, 18–20; indexicality of, 8–9, 27, 29, 36–38, 44, 46–47,

66, 67, 93–94, 103, 109; legacy and, 15–16; nation building and, 51; polysemy of, 36
Pittsburgh Courier (newspaper), 58
postmortem condition, use of term, 15–16

Queen, The (film), 98–99
Quigley, Christine, 18

racial codes, 57
Reagan, Ronald, 122n15
reality television, 107–9
realm of the dead, 1, 3, 81, 87, 103, 110
relics, 12, 40, 53–54, 55–56, 61, 78–79, 105
representational thinking, 49–50, 67, 103
Rowe, Deborah Jeanne, 100

sacrificial lambs, 53, 124n2
Santner, Eric L., 34–35
Scarry, Elaine, 60
Sharpton, Al: eulogy for Jackson, 88, 92–97
Sliwinski, Sharon, 54–55, 80
Southworth, Josiah, 19–20
Spencer, Earl: eulogy for Diana, 88–92, 98, 100
Stalin, Joseph: display of embalmed body, 28
Steinberg, Deborah Lynn, 97
Sterne, Jonathan, 119n26
subjectivity, 2, 3, 4, 5, 12, 23, 24–25, 49, 93
Sullivan, Nikki, 93
symbolic practices, 2
Syrian Free Press, 68

tabloid bodies, 5, 10–11, 81,
83–84, 88–89. *See also* Diana,
Princess of Wales; Jackson,
Michael
thirdness, concept of, 36, 122n23
Thomas, Abriel, 69
Thousand Plateaus, A (Deleuze/
Guattari), 49–50. *See also*
assemblage; hierarchical
thinking; nomadic thinking;
representational thinking
Till, Emmett: civil rights movement
and, 55–61; as martyred
corpse, 5–7, 9, 51, 53–54, 81;
photographs of childhood, 69,
78–79; photographs of corpse,
57, 60, 65–68
torture, 10, 60, 61–62, 67, 70,
73–74, 79, 80–81

United Nations Human Rights
Committee, 64, 74

Unquiet Grave, The
(documentary), 8, 44–49

Vanity Fair (magazine), 85
visuality: in mortuary practices,
14, 17–18; in mourning
practices, 13, 18–19, 27, 30–31,
35. *See also* photography

"We Are ALL Hamza al-Khateeb"
(Facebook page), 10, 63, 75–78,
129n57
white supremacy, 61
William, Duke of Cambridge,
87–88, 97–98, 99
witnessing modality, 85–86,
87
Wittgenstein, Ludwig, 37–38
Wright, Mose, 56–57

Zelizer, Barbie, 12, 76, 119n32,
121n13

Margaret Schwartz is associate professor of communication and media studies at Fordham University.